THE ART OF AGEING

Also by John Lane and published by Green Books:

Timeless Simplicity: creative living in a consumer society
Timeless Beauty: in the arts and everyday life
The Spirit of Silence: making space for creativity
In Praise of Devon: its places, people and character
Devon's Churches: a celebration (with Harland Walshaw)

The Art of
Ageing

*Inspiration for a positive
and abundant later life*

JOHN LANE

with illustrations by Clifford Harper

green books

Published in 2010
by Green Books Ltd
Foxhole, Dartington, Totnes, Devon TQ9 6EB
edit@greenbooks.co.uk www.greenbooks.co.uk

Text © John Lane 2010
Drawings © Clifford Harper 2010

Cover design by Stephen Prior

Text printed by TJ International Ltd, Padstow, Cornwall, UK
on Five Seasons 100% recycled paper

ISBN 978 1 900322 73 7

CONTENTS

ACKNOWLEDGEMENTS

In preparing this book I have acquired a multitude of debts. My first and most substantial acknowledgement must be to Harland Walshaw for editing my text. I am also hugely indebted to Timothy Hyman and Jenny Pearson for reading the manuscript and making many helpful and perceptive criticisms. Barbara Diethelm, Michael Gee, Sue Kellam, Grania Luttman Johnson, Jocelyn Martin, John Moat, Werner Schmidt, and my sons Thomas, Adam, Nathaniel and Jacob, made many invaluable contributions. I am also grateful to those who consented to be interviewed for the 'Brief Lives' chapter of the book. The staff of Great Torrington library have been helpful, as has Philip Gross, who generously granted me permission to use the article about his father, originally published in *The Guardian*.

John Lane
Beaford, Devon
Spring 2010

To my wife Truda
without whose support this book could not have been written

INTRODUCTION

And so, from hour to hour, we ripe and ripe,
And then from hour to hour, we rot and rot.
And thereby hangs a tale.

from *As You Like It* by William Shakespeare

I never knew the world was beautiful
until I reached old age.

Luigi Cornaro

"**N**O YOUNG MAN ever thinks he shall die," observed William Hazlitt, and that was true of me. In my youth I never thought of dying; never wanted to think about age; never for that matter thought of being seriously ill or of taking out any kind of insurance. This was not denial – just a complete lack of interest in the subject. And although I am now in my 80th year, I have rarely been seriously ill – until a few years ago when I was obliged to have a quadruple heart operation and found I had developed Parkinson's disease. Yet even now, bar the occasional urinary problem, constipation and general tiredness, I am reasonably active – so much so that I dared to think that I might even try to write about the subject of this book. For the truth is that for all my grey hairs, sexual impotence, decreased vigour and poor short-term memory, I do not feel old. In spite of all the evidence to the contrary, I largely feel as I have always felt. In this respect I am in sympathy with the attitude of 95-year-old former librarian Jimmy Thirsk. "I ignore old age. I don't believe in it," he said. It is a view, I suspect, shared by the majority of the country's elderly people – at least those continuing to experience reasonably good health.

Ageing remains, of course, a natural part of life, an inevitability. The great whales, the birds of the air, the multitudinous reptiles – all come into being, fall ill, grow old and die, and all of us must sooner or later face the fact that we will do the same. Meanwhile we can only attempt to live with as much grace, delight, imagination and sense of service as we can muster. If we cannot avoid the inevitable, we can at least try to understand, accept and even celebrate the continual flow of life's many transitions. I believe it is precisely the impermanence of life that renders it so precious. Knowing that it is brief requires us to appreciate each moment of beauty and waste no opportunity for learning and love.

Yet how much more difficult this has become because of our culture's glorification of the youthful years. Society devalues the elderly and the lessons that can be learned from maturity, wisdom, pain and loss – even from slowness. Ageing has become the major fear of our generation. Immense sums are being spent to delay its approach. Yet old age continues to advance in a steady progression. In the coming years we will be unavoidably more and more dominated by the elderly. We may or may not be greened by ecological awareness, but we shall certainly be greyed by an ageing population. It has been calculated that by 2040, the number of those in this country over 65 will exceed the number of children under five.

Theodore Roszak's book *America the Wise* takes a positive approach to ageing. He starts with an acceptance of the inevitable fact of an elderly population, but looks forward to the triumph of the old. Their sheer numbers could revolutionise society, moving it from predatory capitalism and environmental exploitation to what Roszak calls "the survival of the gentlest". He argues that the increasing proportion of old people will in time tip the balance in favour of values that they hold dearest: the alleviation of suffering, non-violence, justice, nurturing, and the maintenance of the health and beauty of the planet. To this list I would add the value of sacramental or holy living.

Each of us can help to advance Roszak's vision by exorcising the morbid idea of ageing that can keep older people immobilised by depression, narrowed by anger, and alienated from their calling as elders. To do so we need to see old age in a new light, as neither all bad (sadness, decay and loss), nor all good (as a time of meaning and spirituality), but rather as a complicated mixture of both. Illness and death call forth a variety of emotional responses, ranging from sorrow to horror to light-heartedness and even humour.

This, then, is a book for those facing old age and wondering how to deal with it. In Dante's epic poem, *The Divine Comedy*, Virgil acts as guide, comforter and friend to the author in his long journey through Hell and Purgatory. It is my hope that this book might provide a similar service to those embarking on a very different but no less arduous journey through advancing age.

Before concluding I should like to explain that I am very far from knowing all the answers. I am only a beginner, a learner; someone discovering what works and does not work as I myself age. Nonetheless, one thing I would like to share is this: however difficult life becomes, however closer to extinction we are edging, every moment of consciousness is a precious gift: every sunrise, every patch of grass, every loving human encounter is to be relished with delight and appreciation. Whatsoever you suffer, life is for living and death is the warrant that we are truly alive, that we have been truly here at all. Live it as best you can until it is alas no more!

> Loveliest of trees, the cherry now
> Is hung with bloom along the bough,
> And stands about the woodland ride
> Wearing white for Eastertide.
>
> Now, of my threescore years and ten,
> Twenty will not come again,
> And take from seventy springs a score,
> It only leaves me fifty more.

And since to look at things in bloom
Fifty springs are little room,
About the woodlands I will go
To see the cherry hung with snow.

A. E. Housman

Chapter One

SOME THOUGHTS ON GROWING OLD

Where are the songs of Spring? Ay, where are they?
Think not of them, thou hast thy music too.

John Keats, *Ode to Autumn*

Do not regret growing older. It is a privilege denied to many.

Anon

S O LONG AS our faculties are reasonably sound and we only suffer from the lesser infirmities of advancing age, our final decades can be joyous and fulfilling. Some people may experience bad health, unhappiness and grief, but for many these years can be amongst the happiest they have known – years that provide unequalled opportunities for creative growth enriched by mature relationships with children, grandchildren, spouse or partner and beloved friends.

It is a period which can offer exceptional opportunities. Compared with the restless uncertainties (or hot-headed idealism) of adolescence, it can provide a satisfying stability. Compared, too, with the hectic business of our middle years – usually taken up with the development of family and career – the first years of retirement give us the freedom to explore those ambitions which other preoccupations denied us in the past. As well as increasing physical difficulties, advanced age can bring its own rewards.

It can replace the shallowness of inexperience with a depth of understanding and complexity of being; and restless speed with the serenity of untroubled leisure. Now there is time for experiment and creativity, time for exploring our different potentials, time to live in accordance with our dreams, time to be ourselves.

And as well as this freedom to find a wide range of new interests, ageing has something else to offer: the value of modesty. When the 93-year-old cellist Pablo Casals was asked why he continued to practise his instrument for three hours a day, he wrily replied: "I'm beginning to notice some improvement."

To become an elder is surely (I hope) to grow in wisdom. It is to join the fellowship of those who have found a balance between energy and contemplation, adventure and reflection, enthusiasm and tranquillity. The choice is ours: to become a gloomy pessimist or a life-loving master of the art of living well. "I wanted to live deep and suck out all the marrow of life, so sturdily and Spartan-like as to put to rout all that was not life," writes Thoreau.

As I grow older, thinking about death, through all my melancholy there arises a profound sense of acceptance, a recognition of the fragility and impermanence of life. And let's face it: as Montaigne observed, death is only a few bad moments at the end of life.

Meanwhile, I am relieved to discover that although some faculties are closing down (packing up is probably the better description), other things – inner things – are quietly taking their place. My relationship with the world is shifting from 'outer' to 'inner' concerns. Joy, silence, stillness and contemplation are becoming more important; making, doing and rushing around becoming much less so. As a young man I was immersed in active living – study, work, the pursuit of career and the rearing of children. My attention now has an inward thrust. I love to read, paint, write and listen to music. I find a growing satisfaction in the observation of small things: how the wind is moving through the boughs of a tree, how the tide advances at the water's edge; or the beauty of a scarlet sun sinking behind a bank of grey and violet-coloured cloud. These perceptions, like friendship and the discovery of new knowledge, prove to be deeply nourishing.

Years ago I took delight in travelling. There was my discovery of India, from which I have yet to recover; and the old, the traditional Japan, hardly less stimulating. In different years I have travelled to Russia, Lithuania, Thailand, Morocco, Cambodia, New Zealand, Sweden, Australia and the United States. I now find the contemplation of a few yards of autumnal hedgerow to be enough. Look at the colour of these silvering branches! Look at these ancient white stones and these decaying leaves! Stop to consider the flight of birds settling in the naked branches of a tree and the shining, lacquered surface of a puddle of water. This season's oozy brown, blancmangey mud has its own magnificence. It's December, and the cold wind on my face is a reminder that I am alive!

A similar reconfiguration has occurred, I discover, with respect to my appreciation of works of art. I shall never forget the excitement with which I first heard, say, Alfred Deller's beautiful rendering of Purcell's *Music for a While*. That was wonderful enough, but I now appreciate music with a depth and breadth of knowledge of which I had no understanding at that time. The seed of Purcell has flowered into a Paradise garden of exotic and wonderful blooms.

These late years have also given me yet another freedom: the freedom to be myself, to ignore the confirmation of external approval, to reject today's materialism, its adolescent obsession with fast and excessive living. I like to believe that I have even freed myself from the bondage of conventional behaviour. This is our life, our time, and, within the limits of our responsibilities to others and the environment, it should be enjoyed for its own sake, without constraint from the twin poisons of remorse and guilt.

Nonetheless, getting older is no joke. Ageing takes courage and a stoicism which contrasts with the self-confident and assertive mood of one's earlier years. Ageing is not for the faint-hearted, and anyone who watches the decrepitude of advancing years with a sympathetic eye is often obliged to confess how wretched it can be. "To preside over the disintegration of one's own body, looking on as sight and hearing, strength, speed and short-term memory deteriorate, calls for a heroism that is no less impressive for being quiet and patient," writes Mary C. Morrison.

Although the speed and the degree with which a body deteriorates will vary from person to person, few escape from illness altogether. Other factors can also complicate the passage of old age: the need to downsize, the continuing responsibility towards children, and, perhaps most traumatic of all, the death of close family members. Old people can face financial difficulties, bemoan the deaths of beloved friends and consider without exaggeration that the better part of our lives has already passed.

Yes, it can be a time of sadness and great loss, but also a rewarding period of meaning and spirituality, one that allows each of us to die content in the knowledge that we have at least in part fulfilled the task of becoming the individual we were born to be. There is, of course, no limit to our endeavour to become that person. A full life should have granted us the opportunity to become aware of the lights and shadows, the ascents and descents, the raptures and the disappointments of that tremendous journey.

Depending on who you are, and on the particular gifts with which you have been endowed, your life should have given you at least a handful of opportunities to realise yourself. That, at least, has been my own experience and that of most of my friends. Some have discovered the pleasures of choral singing, digging for archaeological remains, fishing; or, like my mother, helping children to learn to swim. Others have explored bookbinding, photography, ornithology and gardening, or have offered their skills to organisations serving humanitarian, political, religious and cultural causes of many different kinds.

One of my friends is learning to read music, and is taking lessons in singing and in speaking Italian, skills she had always dreamt of being able to practise, but only now has the time and the means to enjoy. Others have found contentment studying a particular subject with the Open University, the Workers' Educational

Association and the University of the Third Age. Yet others have found fellowship and contentment through sport. Rugby and football may no longer be the most suitable physical exercise, but bowls, cricket, croquet, swimming, golf and even tennis are played by many older people, as well as board games, such as chess, which satisfy the competitive urge.

The attractions and responsibilities of a second parenthood keep us in contact with the young and the modern world. There is so much we can learn from our grandchildren. They can help to prevent us becoming grumpy and churlish, and help us adapt to a world very different from the one we knew as children. Being a grandparent is a privilege and a pleasure, and for many it is the principal and most rewarding task of old age, a joy deferred.

There can be no certainty about the life pattern to come and its outcome. Yet whatever occurs, old age is neither all bad nor all good. Like adolescence and other challenging stages of life, it is an uneven mixture of both. "Ageing," writes Thomas Cole, "like illness and death, reveals the most fundamental conflict of the human condition: the tension between infinite ambition, dreams, and desires on the one hand, and vulnerable, limited, decaying physical existence on the other – the tragic and ineradicable conflict between body and spirit. This paradox cannot be eradicated by the wonders of modern medicine or by positive attitudes towards growing old."

William Blake, in his long poem *Auguries of Innocence*, expressed this dualism with perfect concision:

> Man was made for Joy & Woe;
> And when this we rightly know
> Thro' the World we safely go.

Joy & Woe are woven fine,
A Clothing for the Soul divine;
Under every grief & pine
Runs a joy with silken twine.

Chapter Two

A SHORT HISTORY
OF AGEING

*The cause of death is birth, and on your way there
you might want to enjoy things.*

David Hockney

*We already have the statistics for the future:
the growth percentages of pollution, overpopulation, desertification.
The future is already in place.*

Günther Grass

The longevity revolution

Nature is prodigal with life. She is extravagant with birth, encouraging countless more beings to be born than can ever survive to their breeding age, and is no less profligate with death. At least 56 million humans die every year, and half of the small animal and bird population. Creatures as diverse as the blue whale, the praying mantis, the salmon and many species of insect will spawn hundreds of thousands of young for every one that survives. Living to old age in the wild is a rare occurrence. Although it has been said that the Hebrew prophet Methuselah lived for 969 years, the archaeological evidence records that half the men and women of the Neanderthal and Upper Palaeolithic periods died before they were twenty. Only a few lived beyond the age of 50 – Nature or the gods were blamed for accidents, for plague, pestilence, famine and wars. At the time of the Swiss physician Paracelsus (1493-1541), sickness was thought to be the scourge of God.

By the European Middle Ages, the average age of death had risen to about thirty. Food shortages, illness, a poor diet and dirty living conditions all meant that many never experienced longevity. Infectious diseases and accidents – such as drowning, falling, or getting burned by open fires – killed almost half of all children before they were five years old. But those who were tough and lucky enough to reach the age of 20 might hope to live for another 25 years. One of my favourite authors, Michel de

Montaigne (1533-1592), looking back on his youth, saw the age of 30 as the watershed dividing vigour from decline.

From the Bronze Age to the end of the 19th century, life expectancy only grew by an estimated 29 years. Yet since the beginning of the 20th century, in the industrialised world at least, there has been an unprecedented gain of more than 30 years of average life, to over 77.

For the first time in recorded history we are beginning to benefit from a revolution in life-extending medicine and public health. A century or so ago the majority did not live to know their grand-children, but now we can anticipate the prospect of seeing our great-grandchildren. Progress in medicine and in science and technology is leading us to anticipate several decades of uninterrupted leisure. American women now have a life expectancy of 84 years, and men of 81 years. "During any one of those (extra) years," writes Theodore Roszak, "somebody who no longer has to worry about raising a family, pleasing a boss, or earning more money will have the chance to join with others in building a compassionate society where people can think deep thoughts, create beauty, study nature, teach the young, worship what they hold sacred, and care for one another. Once we realise that, we should have no difficulty under-standing the most important fact about the longevity revolution. It has given this remarkable generation the chance to do great good against great odds."

Yet, if a growing population has been regarded as a prime measure of social progress, it is now beginning to be seen as a problem as great as climate change. Today there are four working people for every retired person, and the cost of paying for a decent income for the retired already seems considerable. Yet in 45 years' time there will be just two workers for every retired person. According to Jackie Ashley, writing in *The Guardian*, that's simply impossible. "So what's the answer? Mass euthanasia? Slums for the aged? The importation of millions of young African or Asian people to fill the workforce? Outlandish thoughts, perhaps: but where are the inlandish ones?"

The population explosion

At the same time that increasing numbers are being born, people are also surviving for many more years – into their eighties and nineties, and even longer. Nearly twenty per cent of the population of these islands is now over retirement age, which means that for the first time in our history there are more pensioners than children under the age of 16. In 1952, when Queen Elizabeth came to the throne, she sent 255 celebratory telegrams to every one of her subjects who had attained their hundredth birthday. More than 12,000 are required today.

These figures have been described as a demographic time-bomb. As more and more older people become dependent on a diminishing pool of tax-paying workers, there will be unprecedented consequences for pensions, economies and political systems.

An early warning of the danger of overpopulation was given by the Reverend Thomas Robert Malthus, an English economist and pioneer student of population studies who lived in the midst of the Industrial Revolution, when there were fewer than one billion people in the world. In 1798 Malthus wrote his famous essay *The Principle of Population as It Affects the Future Improvement of Society*, observing that the drain of populations on available resources can be catastrophic, Malthus contended that future poverty was unavoidable because populations increase geometrically, outdistancing the means of subsistence, which can increase only arithmetically.

Malthus's predictions are now much questioned, but we still need to consider how the growing proportion of elderly people is to be supported by a dwindling number of young ones. Could pensions and health care collapse under the unstoppable pressure? Meanwhile James Lovelock and others have argued that we need to bear in mind the likely prospect of global warming being caused by the existence of more people, their pets and their animals than the Earth can comfortably carry. In *The Vanishing Face of Gaia*, he argues that the present world population of some seven billion people is wholly unsustainable and needs to be greatly reduced. "I am not a willing Cassandra and in the past have been publicly sceptical about doom stories, but this time we do have to take seriously the possibility that global heating might all but eliminate people from the Earth."

If these warnings are not enough (and to them must be added the catastrophic impact of resource depletion and environmental degradation), our ancient, irresistible and hubristic yearning for perennial life continues to seduce scientists into seeking solutions to the so-called 'problem' of ageing. Even now plans are being made to develop a substance to slow down the process. *The Independent* (9th July 2009) reports that "Rapamycin, a pharmacological product used to prevent rejection in organ transplants, has been found to extend the lifespan of mice by up to thirty-eight per cent, raising the possibility that it may delay ageing in people . . ." These results are attracting considerable excitement, and an accompanying article in *Nature* by two of the world's leading experts on the ageing process openly asks the question: "Is this the first step towards an anti-ageing drug for people?"

I am with Montaigne, who cautioned his readers that we should not tamper with nature. "She knows her business better than we do," he wrote. I don't imagine that I am alone in my apprehension for the future of our species on this overworked and heavily plundered planet.

The conquest of the old

In the 17th century, capitalism and the industrial mode of production created a revolution in work and thought, politics and markets, culture and leisure, of an immense and continuing impact. Progress and its values demanded not only improved machinery but a new kind of thinking: a new kind of human being.

Kirkpatrick Sale, the author of *Rebels Against the Future*, a study of this revolution, has observed that: "It is in the nature of the industrial ethos to value growth and production, speed and novelty, power and manipulation, all of which are bound to cause rapid and disruptive changes at all levels of society, and with some regularity, whatever benefits they may bring to a few. And because its criteria are essentially economic rather than, say, social or civic, those changes come about without much regard for any but materialist consequences."

They create a society which favours the most adaptable, quick-witted and fast-moving – that is to say the young – rather than their more stable, slower-paced and less enterprising elders, who will find themselves inevitably relegated to second, third and fourth place.

In pre-industrial societies, there was a bias in favour of tradition. Witness the veneration of the old and the preoccupation with death and the hereafter, which have characterised such cultures as the Hindu, the Muslim, the Mexican, the Aboriginal and African, wherein the elderly were valued as the carriers of tradition. They were respected as the stable repositories of customs and legends, the guardians of values, and the experts in all the arts and crafts upon which the community depended for its continuation. An

African proverb says it all: "The death of an old person is like the loss of a library."

What value is knowledge of the past in the context of today's technological society? Knowing how our ancestors did such and such a thing is of little use in our very different world. It can't make money and it won't stimulate employment – rather the reverse.

Before we consider the different contributions which both the young and the old have made in our lifetime, it might be helpful to try to remember the contribution of the elderly in traditional societies. To do so we could start with the wonderful images of North American Indians photographed by Edward S. Curtis in the first decades of the twentieth century. Here we find elders whose voices had authority, whose memories guided the future; men and women characterised by a nobility of bearing and pride in their valued social role.

Another view of the old is to be seen in the work of Rembrandt van Rijn (1606-69), who drew and painted dozens of elderly people, including almost a hundred self-portraits during the course of his career. His are unglamorised portraits; they reveal no evidence of make-up, no hair dye, no face-lifts – only the unvarnished truth that the old can be both beautiful and wise. His portraits may speak of loneliness, but they also register tenderness, peace of mind and a quiet self-esteem. These people knew where they stood and the role they played in society. Consider Rembrandt's *Mother Reading the Bible* of about 1629, a profoundly intimate study of a very old person, her skin as wrinkled as an ancient apple, her mouth toothless and, judging by the large type of the book that she is reading on her lap, nearly blind. Yet it is not these ailments which register her unquestionable authenticity, her nobility as a human being. Unlike the portraits in, say, *Hello!* magazine or *Management Today* (old people rarely feature on television), this portrait is not of a smoothly featured mannequin advertising its marketability, but of a greatly loved and loving human being. The same is true of the wise old man in Rembrandt's wonderful *Simeon in the Temple with the Christ Child*. The dominant mood of both Curtis's photographs and Rembrandt's portraits of old people is one of dignified nobility.

Something of the same quietude and withdrawal from today's ceaseless propaganda in favour of doing is to be discovered in the men and women photographed by Dolf Hartsuiker for his book *Sadhus: Men of India*. The sadhu is of interest here not only because there is nothing like them in the West, but because they are an integral aspect of a culture which has a natural sympathy for the virtues of the aged – a culture which values the freedom to think, to question, reflect and meditate.

Classical Hinduism divides human life into four stages. The first of these two reflects our involvement, as student and householder, with the society into which we have been born: marrying, working and raising a family are examples of this. But when it comes to the later stages of life, the traditional Hindu exchanges the hectic life of his or her youth and middle age for a passive and reflective existence: a life that responds to a slow metabolism and a greatly quietened mind. The elderly sadhus and sannyasis of India (of which there are as many as five million), will choose to live on the margins of society, without possessions, comforts, sensual pleasures and worldly responsibilities; instead they depend on alms, go on pilgrimages and seek what they believe to be the real purpose of existence, Enlightenment. For them, old age is the phase of life which offers the possibility of finding out who they really are. It is the time when they can hope to integrate those parts of themselves which were pushed aside in the race to succeed.

It is therefore obvious that the ambitions of a sadhu are completely out of keeping with the overridingly secular, technological and commercial ambitions of the modern Westerner. Yet I mention them here as an example of how some cultures have chosen to value the importance not only of the spring and summer of our lives, but their autumn and their winter, too – the period of withdrawal, reflection and a search for meaning. In the slow-moving, traditional cultures, old age is usually associated with prudence, sagacity and wisdom: all over Africa, for example, elders continue to be respected and trusted as mediators, facilitators and peacemakers.

Yet when we begin to compare these sentiments with our own society's generally dismissive attitude towards the old, the contrast comes as a shock. While Confucian and Islamic cultures advocate that the old should be treated with special respect, Western society is more inclined to regard them as a problem, even a burden, and sometimes with not much more than a measured tolerance.

According to Robert Butler this attitude can be observed in the current use of the word 'old', which invariably conjures up a negative attitude. "Few people", he writes, "are willing to be identified as aged; 'ageing', 'elderly', 'retired', 'old-timer', 'gramps', 'granny', or even 'old' itself are to be avoided. 'Senior citizen' or 'golden ager' are sugary euphemisms. 'Old fogey', 'old biddy', 'old gal', 'crock' and 'geezer' are putdowns. We can either rehabilitate the least objectionable of these names (perhaps 'elderly' and 'old') to a new and respected status, or we can come up with a new name altogether. The Abkhasians of the Soviet Union solve this problem in a unique manner by describing their elders, as 'long-living' rather than 'old'. The connotation is one of continuing life rather than approaching death."

Rehabilitation of words is one approach, but I prefer, like Jimmy Thirsk, to try to disregard the concept altogether. Yes, old people (including myself) are inexorably moving towards their own physical decline and death. We age, but so do trees, historic buildings, violins and antiques, admired for their patina, their beauty and their very antiquity. As I see it, the denigration of that which is 'old' is simply characteristic of a culture infatuated with the 'new' – with technology, which demands quick-witted adaptability and the other attributes of youth. Or, in the arts, with Modernism, which denigrates tradition and celebrates all that is new.

It is in the nature of the industrial ethos to value this kind of culture – not the stable but the dynamic, not the slow but the fast, not the communal but the individualistic, not the traditional but the novel – all of which fundamentally alters the status of its older members in relation to their successors. We call societies traditional precisely because they are productive communities primarily concerned with the social relations between their members, as opposed to marketplaces that are primarily concerned with economic transactions.

Industrialism, built upon machines, denigrates all that is slow, stable and traditional; the customs and habits of the past are rejected in favour of speed and rapidity of thought. So we lionise the young, making their power, their energy, their sexuality and beauty the standard against which everything else is to be measured. Every new technological invention – the railway, the plane, the mobile phone, the internet, even the microwave – has increased the pressure to live at a faster rate. So now we eat faster and faster (the average time spent in a McDonald's, including ordering and eating, is just 12 minutes), travel faster, cook faster and by texting make contact with one another more quickly than at any time in the past. We also value glamour and sexuality above wisdom and experience. "Waste of time", observes Max Weber in *The Protestant Ethic and the Spirit of Capitalism*, "is the first and in principle the deadliest of sins .... Loss of time through sociability, idle talk, luxury, even more sleep than is necessary for health . . . is worthy of absolute moral condemnation."

It is therefore little wonder that the old are no longer seen as role models. They are tolerated, but viewed as slow, expensive and out of touch, a dead weight on progress and flexibility. In the USA, and to some extent in the UK, this is the heyday of youthful independence; it is the time when vitality is valued, sexuality is celebrated and an exaggerated income is prized above all else. No wonder that some of us will go to any length to camouflage the tell-tale symptoms of decay: wrinkles, weak hearing and grey hair in particular. Any chemist's shop, with its bottles of hair dyes, packets of Viagra and advice about the use of botox, can reveal the scale of the deception that the old are choosing to undertake. Meanwhile young people go their own way, live their own lives, listen to their own music, develop their own relationships (texting is now approaching a mania). Though they do not necessarily neglect their parents, their chief interest lies among those of their own age.

Despite this widespread social prejudice against the elderly, there are signs that attitudes may be changing. In her book *The Fountain of Age*, Betty Friedan observes, "Only recently have maverick gerontologists begun to ask if the long period of age after reproduction might not be as important as that long period of childhood in making us human. . . . Why are we not looking at age as a new, evolving stage of human life – not as a decline from youth, but as an open-ended development in its own terms, which, in fact, may be ours to define?"

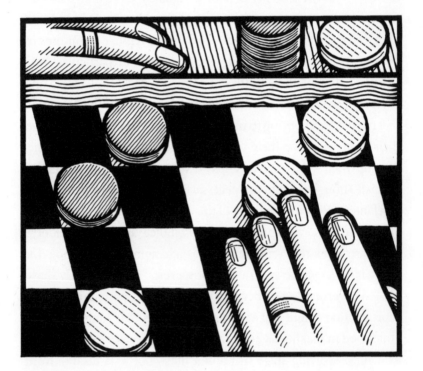

Chapter Three

COPING WITH AGEING

None are so old as those who have outlived enthusiasm.

Henry David Thoreau

Accentuate the positive

To avoid some of the less agreeable aspects of old age, try to live within a positive frame of mind, keep the company of optimistic people and be authentic. No less valuable is the importance of being honest about your dark side, your imperfections. That strikes me as a perfectly good intention, but it's one I've found rather easier to talk about than practise.

In these respects an Indian friend has just written in despair about her 89-year-old father in hospital recovering from major spinal surgery. "It is so exhausting," she exclaims. "My dad is demanding, self-centred and sometimes downright mean. Does old age give you the licence to be bad? If so, why was Gandhi so refined even as he grew older? Is it true that normally altruistic and compassionate people become more selfish in old age, or that habitually selfish people become more selfish as they grow older? "

Since I have neither met my friend's father nor am recovering from spinal surgery, I am barely qualified to answer her questions. Nonetheless, I'd dare to suggest that in general age should not be used as a pretext for selfish behaviour, and that anyone approaching 90 has already left it rather late for serious character reform. My friend would seem to admit this much when she adds: "Talking about old age, it is so, so important to develop the right perspective about it, and work towards the right attitude during one's good years." Yes, to lay the foundations of a wise old age is a long process. So why wait until the end of life to absorb the lessons that could be learned now?

Although anxiety and depression are natural to the human condition, it is advisable to keep them in check. Whenever you discover a mood plunging into negativity, self-abasement or despair, try to reverse the process. Seek to flood your heart with feelings of happiness and joy. Tomorrow is a new day, a new opportunity, so welcome it with gratitude and hope. Let looking forwards, optimism and forgiveness become a way of life for you.

If things are bad, if you are suffering from a life-threatening disease, I know it is damnable, but try to avoid sinking into a condition of self-pitying victimhood: "Why me?" "What have I done to deserve this?" Such thoughts, understandable as they may be, will not help. They do you no good.

Against all the odds, and difficult as it may be, cast your mind towards the wonders that remain for you to enjoy. Relish the moments of glory that exist: this could be the May sun rising through a virgin sky, the glittering radiance of a landscape steaming after a heavy shower, a Schubert song, or the opportunity to enjoy one of Vermeer's wonderful street scenes. Take a look at his painting *The Little Street*: nothing much is happening here. A woman sits in an open doorway absorbed by some handwork; a maidservant busies herself in an adjacent passageway; some children are engrossed by their game as they kneel at the street's edge. This painting is important because it is a timeless record of the poetic beauty of very ordinary everyday life.

It is equally important to overcome what Buddhists describe as attachment. Unlearn the habit, as I have tried (but failed) to do, of judging everything as good or bad. Avoid making judgements of any kind; try not to dwell on problems; strive to be positive. Consider the wonders and advantages of being alive. Instead of ruminating about the emptiness of life, find something to do. Work to heal the residual wounds left from earlier and unsuccessful relationships. Be vigilant that you are not dropping into negativity. It is not what happens but what you make of it that always matters. Be merciful to yourself and others, including animals. Optimism can be learned when you apply yourself to learning it.

Nonetheless, generosity towards oneself should include an appropriate acceptance of what has been lost: strength, vigour, agility, memory, quickness; they may have gone, and gone forever. They had their moments, and we enjoyed them, but now it's the time to go beyond that stage and practise an acceptance of where we are at the present. The denial of ageing is quite simply none other than a rejection of one of the ever-changing processes of life. The fear of ageing can be worse than ageing itself.

Retirement

"And my host uses a curious phrase when he speaks of retiring from business. He calls it 'making his soul'." – Lawrence Durrell

Although retirement offers the possibility of a new life, a fresh beginning, a time for discovery and self-realisation, many of us are ill-prepared by education and past experience for the shock of so much leisure. It is assumed that retirement will give us all that we missed in our previous life: leisure, time, adventure, peace of mind, enchantment. With hopes of that sort in mind, we may set out on a cruise or an escorted tour to some far-flung and exotic destination: Peru, perhaps, or Capri, or down the Niger to Timbuktu, Marrakesh and the Atlas Mountains. But the truth is that although this first cruise or adventure holiday can provide much interest and pleasure, a shot in the arm in dreary February, it is unlikely to be anything more than a temporary fillip.

After the 16-day visit to South Africa, after the weekly game of golf, after watching television, imbibing the nightly tot of whisky and reading the newspaper from cover to cover, there remains not only what to do with the rest of the week, but how to deal with the tens of thousands of hours that have to be filled during the remaining years of life. This is a long time to hang around doing almost nothing.

The lucky ones are those with something significant to do, a consuming interest that needs to be pursued. They are the people who are occupied, who have a purposeful objective, who don't have to consider the question "What shall I do next?" For the key to fulfilment lies in the pursuit of some overriding interest or passion, something that lies above and beyond the merely temporary, however hidden or eccentric it may seem to other people. Some will know what this is without any difficulty. Others may have to dig deep into their very purpose for existence to uncover it.

Finding a way to be useful or interested or amused can take many unexpected forms, as we can see from the following unusual example. It is to be found in the village of Hauterives, in the Department of Drôme in France, where a local postman, Ferdinand Cheval (1836–1924), constructed a unique monument to the imagination, one of the strangest and most moving ever made. Here Cheval describes the origin of his work:

"As a country postman, like my 27,000 comrades, I walked each day from Hauterives to Tersanne – in the region where there are still traces of the time when the sea was here – sometimes going through snow and ice, sometimes through flowers. What can a man do when walking everlastingly through the same setting except dream? I built in my dreams a palace passing all imagination, everything that the genius of a simple man can conceive – with towers, castles, museums and statues: all so beautiful and graphic that the picture of it was to last in my mind for at least ten years. . . .

"When I had almost forgotten my dream, and it was the last thing I was thinking about, it was my foot which brought it all back to me. My foot caught on something which almost made me fall: I wanted to know what it was: it was a stone of such strange shape that I put it in my pocket to admire at leisure. The next day, passing through the same place, I found some more, which were even more beautiful. I arranged them together there and then on the spot and was amazed. . . . I searched the ravines, the hillside, the most barren and desolate places. . . . I found tufa which had been petrified from water, which is also wonderful. . . .

"This is where my trials and tribulations began. I then brought along some baskets. Apart from the thirty kilometres a day as a postman, I covered dozens with my basket on my back full of stones. Each commune has its own particular type of hard stone. As I crossed the countryside I used to make small piles of these stones: in the evenings I returned with my wheelbarrow to fetch them. The nearest were four to five kilometres, sometimes ten. I sometimes set out at two or three in the morning."

Such was Cheval's obsession that he worked alone on his creation for 33 years. Such a man has no need to consider retirement or go on a cruise to Peru.

Another remarkable instance of a fulfilling involvement in late years is that of the reclusive, semi-literate Cornish rag-and-bone man, Alfred Wallis (1855-1942), who took up painting at the age of seventy, after the death of his wife, "for company". Completely untutored, Wallis continued to paint on old scraps of cardboard, mostly oddly shaped, supplied by the local grocer. He insisted on using ships' paint, a medium which he understood. His subject was usually the sea and boats – scenes he had known as an Atlantic fisherman in his youth – and the landscape of St Ives, where he lived. He was discovered by the artists Christopher Wood and Ben Nicholson, who were profoundly influenced by his work, but he sold his pictures for just a few pence, nailing them to the door of his shop. Wallis died in the workhouse at the age of 87, and is buried in a pauper's grave. He is now recognised as one of the greatest primitive painters of the 20th century, and his paintings can be seen hanging in the Tate at St Ives.

Each of us is born with a unique talent, one we have lived with and will die with, realised or unrealised. To my mind, one of life's purposes is to discover and fulfil this capacity, to bring it to flower as an expression of our genius.

Erich Fromm asks, "What is the opposite of the consumer? What is the opposite of the empty, passive person who spends – or as I would say, wastes – his life by killing time?

"This is very difficult to describe, but I would say, in a general way, the main answer is to be interested."

Stress

Although, of course, a situation that is stressful for one person may not be so for another, too much stress can be harmful for anyone. A degree of stress is probably acceptable; it can occur when the demands of children, lack of money, poor health and emotional problems become not merely uncomfortable but unbearable. We may all suffer during those times when the pressure of work becomes simply overpowering; but they are usually short-lived. However, it's not always the personal that erodes equanimity. The impersonality, competitiveness, individualism and frenetic pace of contemporary life also induce stress and, for that matter, other emotional problems. Rates of depression have been found to be significantly greater today as compared with 20 to 40 years ago. Rates of suicide and divorce have also increased since 1950.

Our society is characterised by an exceptional number of features which generate anxiety. The daily press, the internet, radio and television are only too prepared to bring to our attention the catastrophes that afflict the world, both natural and man-made: war, famine, drought, pestilence, flood, earthquake, volcanoes, melting glaciers, global warming, drug-dependence, overpopulation, child abuse, plagues of locusts – all make for dramatic headlines. The beneficial aspect of all this publicity is that it can tap into a well of generosity which restores your faith in humanity, and brings desperately-needed relief to the afflicted in all parts of the world. But some will find the concentration on tragedy to the exclusion of any good news a source of personal depression and anxiety.

Experienced in moderation, stress can be of real value as a warning, a stimulus, even a challenge, but too much stress can encourage the symptoms of ageing.

One 'answer' to stress (if there is an answer) is the regular and conscious development of a relaxation response, which could be nothing more than the stroking of a beloved pet, the practice of meditation, yoga, and working with your breath. Other forms of relaxation (such as taking biofeedback training, floating in water, walking in nature, listening to beautiful music) can also prove effective. Beauty is one of life's most wonderful healers – completely accessible and free of charge. Creativity animates every aspect of human life, and tranquillity can be found when you search for it.

Whereas beauty always nourishes the soul, ugliness will besmirch it with its lovelessness. Ugliness makes us ill; it depresses rather than exalts. It should be avoided like a plague of locusts.

Guilt

Look into the eyes of a young child and you discover that they have not yet been jaded by life. They have no cynicism or malice. They do not have enough references to judge harshly. They do not carry grudges and, in most cases, their lives remain undistorted by negativity, fear and guilt.

Guilt, learnt in childhood, is an especially corrosive blight, difficult to throw off and, as David Kessler says, a connection to our weakness, our shame, and not having been forgiven. "When we feel guilty, we stay small-minded, our lower thoughts are in control."

Try sharing your guilt; confess it and forgive yourself. Do not live according to what you should do, but how you really are. Be honest about who you are and neither exaggerate your perfections nor your imperfections.

Fear

At its best, fear can be a valuable warning system which puts us on guard against the genuine possibility of trouble. More likely it will have a seriously debilitating effect – an effect which causes anxiety and a sense of failure. "Fear is a shadow," writes Elizabeth Kübler-Ross, "that blocks everything: our love, our true feelings, our happiness, our very being."

The reality is that although it might, your house will not necessarily burn down, and that the aircraft in which you are travelling will not necessarily crash. But there is no might about the fear of death, which in all probability is at the root of all the other lesser fears. So what is to be done? Learning to face the fear of death is the only way to transcend and conquer it. Elizabeth Kübler-Ross writes: "To transcend fear, we must move somewhere else emotionally; we must move into love. . . . Infusing ourselves with love begins the washing away of our fears. . . . Practise doing the small things that you are afraid of doing. Your fear only holds enormous power over you when not challenged. Learn to use the power of love and kindness to overcome fear. . . . It is fear itself that brings us so much unhappiness in life, not the things we fear."

Anger

Anger can range from mild irritation to violent rage. It can be a normal, healthy and even helpful reaction to a temporary annoyance, insult or injustice. In our sometimes impersonal and business-dominated society, situations arise which induce, shall I say, a considerable annoyance. Seeking an answer to a small enquiry, I am obliged to press numbers on a telephone, listen to a rigmarole about data protection, endure Vivaldi's *Four Seasons* being played for the umpteenth time and no less frequently be told that my call really matters. But, of course, the source of anger can be much more serious, rooted in affront, lack of respect, insult and hurt pride. Once the fuse has been lit, it can lead to damaged relationships, self-hurt and even violence against others.

Bear in mind that anger rarely heals, and can worsen a poor situation. It may produce a temporarily pleasurable energising effect – the seduction of adrenalin has its own attraction. But it is usually better to remain uninvolved, to keep silent. Of course, a sustained grudge can be psychologically damaging, and to release your feelings with an occasional angry outburst may act as a safety valve. But if you are constantly blaming yourself and others, if you are often irritable, humourless and short-tempered, then you probably need help and advice. It can be difficult to recognise these traits in yourself. Listen to what others say about you, and do not hide behind an impenetrable shield of self-righteousness, and a determination to win at all costs.

This is a complicated subject, not easily summarised here, and there are many books about the subject that could be consulted.

Money

Various factors are known to help or hinder the quality of life in our later years, and of these our state of health and level of income are possibly the most important. Yet variations between persons, cultures and families are so great that it is virtually impossible to draw neat conclusions. Nonetheless, although some people have put aside sufficient savings to tide them over any shortfall or can depend on the help of a good pension, this is not always the case; after retirement some can find themselves obliged to manage with much less than they were formerly used to spending. In these circumstances they may be obliged to live on a reduced income and even move to cheaper accommodation.

It is a mistake to assume that this will be a disaster. The evidence points to the fact that once a certain level of material sufficiency has been reached, increasing prosperity does not inevitably induce a commensurate rise in well-being. There are large swathes of the rich who say they are unhappy, and large swathes of the poor who say they are happy. Subjective satisfaction does not necessarily accord with objective circumstances.

Becoming aware

Awareness makes a difference in ageing. Although every one of the many millions of the Earth's species is ageing, it is only the higher forms of animal which seem to be aware of what is happening to them; who comprehend, that is, the possibility of non-existence. When death occurs, the African elephant is solemn and touchingly mournful at the loss. For days after a death a family of elephants can stand round the dead body, touching it gently with their trunks and covering the body with leaves and twigs.

For humans, to despair of growing old and dying has been seen to induce a quickening rate of ageing. To accept the cyclical nature of life with grace may even help to keep some miseries, both physical and mental, from the door. The commonsense notion that 'you're only as old as you think you are' contains much truth in it.

The consumer society

We live in a certain kind of society – a mass society and a consumer society – which for all its benefits, including high levels of comfort, income and 'leisure', extracts a heavy price. Many work at jobs which, in the words of the writer Studs Terkel, are "too small for the human spirit".

The psychologist Erich Fromm has something to say on the consequences of this situation. "The average man today", he writes, "may have a good deal of fun and pleasure, but in spite of this he is fundamentally depressed. Perhaps it clarifies the issue if instead of using the word 'depressed' we use the word 'bored'. Actually there is little difference between the two, except a difference in degree, because boredom is nothing but the experience of a paralysis of our productive powers and the sense of aliveness. Among the evils of life there are few which are as painful as boredom, and consequently every attempt is made to avoid it."

There are many advantages to living a less cluttered, stressful life, in which one may have fewer things but more time to enjoy creative activities, more time just to be. My previous book *Timeless Simplicity: creative living in a consumer society* discusses these issues in some depth.

Chapter Four

DELAYING THE ADVENT OF OLD AGE

*To know how to grow old is the masterwork of wisdom
and one of the most difficult chapters in the great art of living.*

Henri Amiel

A LTHOUGH WE CANNOT OVERCOME the inherent nature of old age, which no amount of vitamins or de-wrinkling cream can ever rectify, it may be possible to transcend some of its infirmities through attitudes and behaviour. In this spirit the following observations, far from new, may be of some value.

Healthy living

I am not qualified to discuss the best way to extend the duration of life from a medical point of view. Nonetheless a great deal of research has been undertaken to establish how we might seek to live as long as possible. In the 1930s, the writer Maurice Ernest in *The Longer Life* examined the biographies of centenarians across many European cultures and back to ancient times. Ernest concluded that practising just a few physical processes would extend our lives to 100 or 120 years. He gave the following prescriptions:

Eat frugally
Exercise and get plenty of fresh air
Choose a congenial occupation
Develop a placid or easy-going personality
Maintain a high level of personal hygiene
Drink wholesome liquids
Abstain from stimulants and sedatives
Get plenty of rest
Have a bowel movement once a day

Live in a temperate climate

Enjoy a reasonable sex life

Get proper medical attention in case of illness

Deepak Chopra (to whom I am indebted for the above information) extends the subject by relating the story of the 15th-century Venetian nobleman Luigi Cornaro, who is famed in gerontology because he resolved, after a roaringly dissolute youth, to pursue a healthy course of life, and try to live until at least one hundred years. "He succeeded spectacularly. In an age where the average person was fortunate to live to 35, Cornaro lived to 103 and remained active and clear-headed to the end. His method for achieving this feat was to abstain from drinking alcohol and to eat very sparingly." In essence, his diet consisted of bread, meat, and broth with eggs, following ancient Greek and Roman notions that a frugal diet is the secret of longevity. In his book *Discourses on the Temperate Life*, Cornaro argues that, contrary to the popular belief that life for the elderly is unattractive, "I never knew the world was beautiful until I reached old age."

Further guidance comes from a remarkable study of 5,820 men of Japanese descent. Since 1965, when they were an average 54 years old, the surviving men now range from 85 to 105. This study repeats many of the factors already listed, and uncovers a further six significant pointers towards a healthy old age: no smoking, no more than two alcoholic drinks a day, normal blood pressure and blood sugar, the avoidance of overweight and the maintenance of physical strength. The healthiest men are non-smoking, strong, lean, and moderate drinkers with normal blood sugar and blood pressure. Physical exercise is one of the most important ways that we can make a difference to our health.

Food, exercise and rest

There is no doubt that a good diet (including certain dietary supplements) and proper physical exercise can play a critically important role in the maintenance of a healthy body and, in consequence, the possibility of an extended life. Walking is an especially important activity, but such exercise-related activities as yoga, pilates and Tai Chi are equally beneficial and eminently suitable for older people. But to do this subject the justice it requires, I urge the reader to consult books such as Andrew Weil's *Healthy Eating: A Lifelong Guide to your Physical and Spiritual Well-Being*.

Of no less importance than exercise is sleep. People who nap generally enjoy better mental health. It should be borne in mind that early peoples (and 'primitive' tribesmen and women today) apparently took more leisure and rest than we do, for all our so-called labour-saving devices. For these peoples, all forms of recreation – music making, self-decoration, communal dancing and the telling of the ancient tribal stories – were highly regarded. In contrast, the strains of travel, employment (or unemployment), existential anxiety and the like are causing serious levels of stress in our time.

Humour

The gift of humour is one of the most important we can hope for. It can liberate us from the narrow prison of our ego, act as a lubricant in relationships and lighten occasions and conversation. Laughter also helps us physically. Scientific studies reveal that it reduces stress and triggers the release of substances called endorphins, which can elevate one's mood. A recent study at Loma Linda University in California suggests that laughter can unleash the same changes in the body's chemistry as a quick bout of physical exercise.

Prolonged laughter, it is claimed, can lower blood pressure and boost immune activity. Of course, seriousness plays a significant role in every life, but it should be reserved for really important matters, leaving the inconsequential ones for a lighter touch. Whenever possible try to introduce a note of laughter. Even when dealing with a subject as sombre as death, humour can have its place.

It may be of interest to note that the person with the longest lifespan recorded beyond reasonable doubt, a Frenchwoman called Jeanne Calment, who died at the age of 122, attributed her long life to her sense of humour. She smoked until she was 110!

The Life Review

Nothing can be more instructive than the desire, common among older people, to look back on life and assess past projects, problems, relationships, successes and failures. You might consider keeping a journal – not so much an account of daily doings as an honest scrutiny of your inner life – the thoughts, dreams, ambitions, attitudes and responses to what is happening to you. Ask yourself: how am I coping with the inevitable diminishment of my physical and intellectual life? How do I react to being sidelined by those who are younger, more vigorous and probably less experienced than I am? Is this the moment to take a back seat and give up making all the decisions? To what extent am I seeking to be who I am not? Have I made wise use of my time on earth? Have I managed to strike a balance between time for myself and time for other people? What are the attributes I have most valued in myself? What is the main source of joy in my life, and has it been given sufficient attention?

Sex

Although Chinese medicine has long recognised the importance of sexuality for health, longevity and spirituality, the majority of older people experience a precipitous drop in the frequency of sexual activity as they age. Of course, cuddling, fondling and masturbation do not necessarily cease, but with exceptions, sexual activity becomes of less importance as we age. Do I miss it? Yes of course I miss its excitement, but less than I might have supposed in the virile physicality of youth.

As you age and the fleshly pleasures lose their erotic appeal, spiritual pleasures become increasingly attractive. Those which have especially delighted me are the pleasures of friendship, nature, the arts and personal creativity, but other people will no doubt be exploring a different set of enchantments.

The importance of a goal

Life without meaning is empty, but meaning is something you must find for yourself. It is not for anyone else to tell you what your life is about. To make sense, it needs a purpose, but it should always be your purpose, rather than one legitimised and dictated by popular opinion in the media, advertising and the unreflective consumerism of our commercial culture.

Therefore, take time to explore and define your life's purpose. Despite infirmity and adversity, continue to search for the golden thread which may provide answers to the ultimate question – what is the role and purpose of your existence? When you discover that mission and commit yourself to it, your life will be more fulfilled. The importance of goal is emphasised by the philosopher Nietzsche, who wrote, "He who has a why to live for can bear almost any how."

Nothing is more energising, more essential, than a life purpose which provides the motivation for living. The 80-year-old American painter Robert Motherwell puts it this way. "One wonderful thing about creativity is that you're never satisfied with what you're trying to do. . . . For me to retire from painting would be to retire from life." Another painter, David Hockney, finds himself busier than ever at the age of 73. Currently working in preparation for the most ambitious exhibition of his life, he says he has more energy than he had ten years ago. "I'll always run up the stairs, especially for a cigarette."

"Woe to him," adds Viktor Frankl, who survived his years in Auschwitz, "who sees no more sense in his life, no aim, no purpose, and therefore no point in carrying on. He is soon lost. The typical reply with which such a man rejected all encouraging arguments was, 'I have nothing to expect from life any more.' What sort of answer can one give to that?"

A case in point is to be found with perhaps the 20th century's greatest writer, Marcel Proust (1871-1922), a lifelong invalid who struggled to complete his sixteen-volume novel À la Recherche du Temps Perdu before his death. It took him ten years to complete the task. According to his biographer, Jean-Yves Tadie, it was in the spring of 1922 that Proust, smiling and looking weary, summoned his housekeeper, Céleste, to announce: "I have important news. Tonight, I wrote the word 'end'. Now I can die." And a few months later he did.

A programme of daily renewal

Take time every day to practise at least one activity that makes you feel energised, be it bathing, walking, reading, writing letters, listening to music, yoga, gardening, or simply breathing. The feeling of repose and renewal that you experience when you are most deeply yourself can be a profoundly liberating experience.

Consider making a corner – a kind of altarpiece of chosen and potent objects: perhaps some stones, a few dried flowers, a photograph, a memento from a journey – where, when you contemplate it, you can be most deeply yourself.

The great psychologist Carl Jung set about creating a more ambitious place of renewal, a second home expressing in physical form his inner nature. He built this himself at the edge of Lake Zurich, a round tower called Bollingen. "I have done without electricity, and tend the fireplace and stove myself. Evenings, I light the old lamps. There is no running water, and I pump water from the well. I chop the wood and cook the food. These simple acts make man simple; and how difficult it is to be simple. . . . There I see life in the round, as something forever coming into being and passing on."

Sustaining the spirit

There are many pleasures, including all the sensual ones – eating, sex, napping and the relief of pain. Montaigne, ever realistic, even mentions the passing of a kidney stone (a problem from which he frequently suffered), but for some the most life-giving experiences are aspects of the play instinct. Of course, this involves the whole of sport (football, cricket, swimming, sailing, golf, billiards, tennis and games such as bridge, chess and draughts) but it can also include the idea of playful living. Of this the poet W. B. Yeats wrote, "Only when we are gay over a thing, and can play with it, do we show ourselves its master, and have minds clear enough for strength."

I therefore suggest the value of maintaining a light-hearted, playful, creative and flexible attitude to all things in your life. Creativity is our birthright; without it we are not fully alive, and are certainly unfulfilled. But at this point it may be helpful to understand that creativity is not necessarily limited to those who are considered Artists with a capital A – poets, composers, painters, dancers and the like – but is better regarded as an integral part of all the simple acts of daily life. Why not explore one or other of these different forms of creativity?

There is, for example, cooking: a deeply satisfying occupation that too many men have sometimes left to the women in their lives ("I can't even boil an egg," I've heard them so often boast). But for people who have retired and have time on their hands, cooking is the perfect recreation. It is an opportunity to experiment with new ingredients, exciting combinations of colour, interesting textures, unusual recipes. It is also an opportunity to invite friends and neighbours into your home.

Today there are many excellent books to guide you into the preparation of delicious food: begin with dishes such as soups, risotto, pancakes, salads, curries, vegetable stews, pastas and simple desserts. But resist the temptation to purchase processed foods, and ignore all the propaganda that food preparation is essentially tedious. Yes, it's true that there are aspects of housekeeping that are monotonous, but this is the case of any job, indeed of any creative pursuit. Frozen and prepared foods may be of occasional value, but their use always cuts us off from the truly pleasurable, creative side of life.

Breadmaking is another deeply satisfying craft, and not necessarily hard work; the Grant loaf which my wife has been making for decades does not take hours of kneading. There's a special magic in adding some yeast to a pile of flour, and turning it into a risen loaf. Eaten warm with home-made marmalade or a good local cheese, it comes as close to gastronomic perfection as you can find in this world.

Then another wonderful activity: gardening. I know of several old people for whom gardening is a lifeline to delight – an activity demanding skill, providing interest and beauty, and for all of them a place of quiet retreat. Individuals derive huge benefit from regular work in their gardens. A garden brimming with beans, aubergines, courgettes, cauliflowers, lettuces, tomatoes, cucumbers, potatoes, beetroot and cabbage is not only a source of healthy nutrition but a special delight in its own right.

For many older people allotments – besides providing a chance to grow food and keep fit – are a wonderful place to meet others and make new friends.

Putting problems in perspective

Yes, we may have problems. We may have difficulty sleeping, and at times can barely walk without pain; but it is important not to lose sight of the scale of these difficulties in relation to the unimaginable suffering of those who are more deeply afflicted throughout the world – those who are starving, those who are suffering from permanent pain, those whose anguish is all but intolerable.

Another perspective is to consider our difficulties in the context of the unimaginable scale of the Creation. There is the Milky Way with its 300,000 million stars. There is the nearest fixed star, which is about 25 million million miles away. Consider, too, the wonder of nature: the 228 separate and distinct muscles in the head of a caterpillar. This world in which we find ourselves is an unimaginable mystery, to which we can only respond with awe and a sense of worshipful attention.

The value of doubt

The Buddhist thinker Ajahn Chah reflects that any speech which ignores uncertainty is not the speech of a sage. Nothing is permanent. Nothing is fixed. Remember, too, that certainty blocks the way forwards, whereas uncertainty offers a fresh creative opportunity.

He also advises us to consider the question "Why was I born?" and to do so frequently, in fact several times a day.

Gratitude

Whenever you stop to listen at the counter of a shop, you cannot but notice the ceaseless employment of the phrase 'thank you'. But courtesies of this order, the small talk of social intercourse, are of a different order from the deep-seated gratitude expressed by poets such as Gerard Manley Hopkins, Walt Whitman and Thomas Traherne in their ecstatic prose and poetry. Such writing is the purest form of love, for when you feel gratitude there is rarely room for a negative response – recrimination, anger, revenge, self-pity.

Find contentment with what you have and be grateful for it. Forget the troubling but petty problems of everyday life and look around with appreciation. Reciprocate your delight by seeking opportunities to act with gratitude. Be thankful for the opportunity to be alive.

Do not be drawn towards the bad. Do not allow yourself the attraction of despair. Look for the honest, the beautiful and the good.

Enjoying the small, unassuming pleasures

Enjoy the modest pleasures that remain. These include friendships, walking, gardening, cooking, eating, writing poetry, painting, playing bowls, listening to and playing music; and for those who are physically disabled, napping, sitting in silence and reading. Domestic animals also contribute their own quiet benediction, and trees their groundedness and peace. As our physical faculties weaken, such acts as tying shoelaces can take on a growing significance. We may find satisfaction in the completion of the smallest task and thereby develop a greater sense of the preciousness of life.

Take time to be silent and to meditate. There is no rush, there are no deadlines, there is no appointment to be made. We can relish what lies about us, whether in the street outside the house, the garden, or the living-room.

Just looking, just listening, just paying attention to what is; this provides a timeless nourishment. There is always cause for gratitude and thanksgiving.

Acceptance

One of the keys to a fulfilling life is the acceptance of whatever is happening to you. Accept that your muscles are weakening, that every act takes longer, that you are less focused than you used to be. Some activities I once took for granted are now beyond my grasp. They will never return, and it is pointless to mourn them. So it's foolish to pretend to be young when you are no longer so. Think young, but with dignity.

Without undue and needless complacency, approve of yourself and take pride in your achievements. Also remember to respect your ageing body, not as a servant but as a friend. It requests no recognition, but offers you its service, so listen to its needs and do not abuse it. Whatever you suffer, retain your human dignity. Dostoevsky said, "There is only one thing that I dread: not to be worthy of my sufferings." Resignation, stoicism and patience serve the ageing well. Watch out for the least sign of self-pity, and ignore the unreasonableness of your plight, the injustice of your illness. It is, and that's that.

Be positive in all things. Accept that life moves on. Enjoy what remains and never ever lose sight of the indescribable mystery which lies behind, beyond and within existence. This is the mystery that sings in all things and can only be experienced with a heart open to the new. Einstein wisely said, "He to whom this mystery is a stranger and can no longer pause to wonder and stand rapt is as good as dead."

Power over ageing

"Nothing holds more power over the body than our beliefs, which influence every cell of the body. It is not our genes but our beliefs that control our lives," says Bruce Lipton, author of *The Biology of Belief*. He writes that positive thoughts are a biological mandate for a happy, healthy life. In the words of Mahatma Gandhi:

Your beliefs become your thoughts
Your thoughts become your words
Your words become your actions
Your actions become your habits
Your habits become your values
Your values become your destiny

Hundreds of research findings from the last three decades have verified that ageing is more dependent on the individual than was ever dreamed of in the past. "All that we are", taught the Buddha, "is the result of our thoughts; it is founded on our thoughts; made up of our thoughts; human beings can alter their lives by altering their attitudes of mind." But, of course, the degree to which this is possible will depend on the will, vitality, determination and courage of the person concerned.

Try to become aware of the thought patterns that determine your behaviour. So long as there is hope and love, we can anticipate living for a longer period than when lives have been corroded with despair.

The stark truth is that, for some, dying offers the only escape from an unfulfilling life. Yet a life enriched with faith and creativity offers the prospect of further living. People cling to life when something dear is at stake, but relinquish it as soon as they see that there is nothing left to live for.

Pets

Florence Nightingale, when writing about the role of music in facilitating recovery from illness, observed that companion animals have a natural place in the sickroom and can do much to alleviate the loneliness which comes with a long convalescence. This is true. Watching the behaviour of cats and dogs will always bring delight. One of my oldest friends – a bachelor in his 86th year – has found important life-giving companionship in caring for his cat – a (spoilt) Mr Tumness. Of this kind of loving relationship Jeffrey Masson observes: "The cat does not merely experience contentment, he exudes it. You cannot be in the presence of a contented cat and not have some of that contentment rub off on you. Which surely is a good part of the reason we love cats so. Scientists have observed that petting a purring cat lowers our blood pressure. I believe it can raise our morale at the same time. Why is this? To feel needed and appreciated by a creature who seems so self-possessed, apparently needing nothing beyond his own perfect self, can be very cheering. 'I can't be all that bad, if my cat likes me so much.'"

Dogs can also be important to older people, especially to those living alone. They are the greatest companions and have the added benefit of getting you out on walks. But older people need to choose the right dog and remember that one you acquire at 65 might still be needing long walks at 75.

The budgerigar is another creature whose happy chattering brings delight to the lonely.

Learning to use a computer

Although I have come close to suicide because my computer is so perversely difficult to use, it can, once mastered, play an important role in your life. The internet enables you to share interests and make contact with people all around the world. Cyberspace provides you with a different way of maintaining connections in older age.

Being adaptable and creative

As we become older there can arise a tendency to resist change and shut out the world around us. It is essential to avoid this, to keep open your curiosity, your delight, flexibility and innate creativity.

Someone who does not feel creative, but useless, stale, a burden to others, can hardly help feeling bored, dull and depressed.

Accepting dependence

Although most of us usually welcome opportunities to help other people with their difficulties, it also happens that dependence – needing assistance – makes some people uncomfortable. We prefer to stand on our own feet, remain independent and self-sufficient. This in general is, of course, a good thing so long as it is not carried to extremes. It is unwise to let feelings of humiliation stand in the way of the grateful acceptance of an offer of help.

Looking outwards

For many old people, whether they continue their life's work or seek entirely new activities, the key to finding meaning in old age can be involvement with other people, with the community. Muriel Gillick, referring to The MacArthur Foundation Study of Successful Aging, found that 80 per cent of older Americans agreed that "life is not worth living if one cannot contribute to the welfare of others." It would appear that if we are to triumph over stagnation and self-absorption and enjoy a contented old age, we need to look outside ourselves and have a concern for the next generation. Nonetheless, 'involvement with community' does not necessarily imply doing something as demanding as running a youth club or even, as I once did, a Scout group. There are many other possibilities, such as shopping for a bedridden neighbour, projecting films at the local arts centre, raising funds for the parish church, serving on the management committee of a charity, and so forth.

Looking inwards

The last years of our lives provide us with opportunities for reflection on what it has all been about; an active consideration of the deep and deepest questions – who we are and where we might fit into the whole, vast, scheme of things.

Slowing down is the way to take advantage of this need. Sitting in stillness and alone is for some a necessary prelude to when the final moment comes. "Many old men and women", writes Irene Claremont de Castillejo, "are cheated of their essential solitude, and kept continually focused on outer things by the mistaken kindness of the young and their lack of awareness of the need to be alone. We die alone. It is well to become accustomed to being alone before that moment comes."

As you age and the fleshly pleasures lose their appeal, spiritual pleasures become the more attractive.

Being yourself

Make no mistake, it requires courage to stand out from one's contemporaries and be totally yourself. It is said that Henry David Thoreau's neighbours saw him stand motionless for as long as eight hours beside a pond to observe young frogs, and all day at a river's edge to watch some duck eggs hatching. Something similar has been reported about the poet Gerard Manley Hopkins, and it goes without saying that other great observers – Gilbert White, Leonardo da Vinci, John Constable, Pierre Bonnard – found fulfilment and delight in their patient, grateful contemplation of the natural world which surrounded them.

Staying young

If you want to stay young it is a good idea to imbibe the flexibility and dynamism of the young. I know that it's not always easy, but try to do so; find opportunities to interact with them. Find out what their dreams and problems are, what they are thinking. Whatever happens, keep young in spirit.

If you feel stuck, have patience and look at things from a fresh perspective. Be prepared to abandon old positions which have ceased to contribute anything of importance. Change, at least in moderation, is valuable; if we do not remain open to it we will not be able to remain open to life. However much we may wish it to be otherwise, life is never under our personal control.

The maintenance of hope

We can have hope even when we know that our survival is hopeless. It is the one human attribute that we would be wise to keep alive in all circumstances. If you lose your partner or a dear friend, do not let grief paralyse the heart. Keep going while you can, but have mercy on yourself. Even when things are not going well, try to force yourself to explore new opportunities or ways of improving your life.

In this chapter I have presented a few ideas which could help you to delay the ageing process. But you too, like the countless others who have preceded us, will almost certainly one day be old and find yourself sick and frail. Eating nutritious food and exercising on a regular basis can certainly help us to remain healthy, but ageing is inevitable and we should try to make the most of this natural process. To be alive is to age.

Chapter Five

YOUR ONE WILD
AND PRECIOUS LIFE

Lord, we know what we are but know not what we might become.

Ophelia, in *Hamlet*, Act 4.

My soul, do not yearn for immortality, but exhaust the realms of the possible.

Pindar (518-438 BC), *Pythian Odes*, III.109

An aged man is but a paltry thing.
A tattered coat upon a stick, unless
Soul clap its hands and sing and louder sing
For every tatter in its mortal dress

W. B. Yeats

AT THE TURN of the last century, life expectancy was broadly defined in terms of the Biblical three score years and ten. That long-accepted measure has now ceased to have any relevance. For the first time in human evolution we, the present generation, have to consider how to spend an additional 20 or more years of relatively active life. We have to reflect on how we can use these years in new and productive ways. "Tell me", asks the contemporary American poet Mary Oliver, "what it is you plan to do/ with your one wild and precious life?" Yes, tell me, what are you planning? Not, I trust, just sitting around watching television, reading newspapers and drinking endless cups of tea. Or, as some of my friends are doing, endlessly travelling. We get from life in the measure with which we give to it, and our fundamental growth – and delight – demands imagination, selective choice and effort.

Old men ought to be explorers

This book has been written in the belief that, as the poet T.S. Eliot urged us to remember, "Old men ought to be explorers/ Here or there does not matter." I take this to include old women. I also take it that Eliot is urging us to make the most of our remaining years, years not infrequently impeded by ill health. That is to say, to follow curiosity, enquire into important ideas, have the courage to go on growing, to be creative and contribute to the society into which we have been born. Or, to put it in another way, to seek to develop fresh mental and imaginative horizons beyond those with which we are already familiar. Those who have done this, who have allied themselves with the creative force that lies at the core of the universe, are my inspiration. I think here of my beloved William Blake in his 70th year, bedridden and sick, yet producing some of his most remarkable work – having taught himself Italian, he paints a series of watercolours based on Dante's great poem *The Divine Comedy*. Then there is the composer Ralph Vaughan Williams, setting out at the age of 85 to write his ninth symphony. And Claude Monet, creating some of his most original paintings up to a month before his 86th year.

Centuries ago the story was similar: the Venetian painter Titian was producing wonderful work at the age of 99; the Florentine sculptor, poet and painter Michelangelo was sculpting his *Pieta* within a few days of his death aged 90, and Sir Christopher Wren was refining his design for St Paul's Cathedral until the very end of his life.

Other remarkable instances of creativity at a late age include the Florentine sculptor Donatello, still working in his 80th year; Germany's greatest poet, Johann Wolfgang von Goethe, who finished *Faust Part II* the year before his death, aged 83; Victor Hugo, author of *Les Misérables* and *The Hunchback of Notre Dame*; and Leo Tolstoy, the author of *War and Peace*; both working until the end of their long lives. Of musicians, Giuseppe Verdi wrote *Falstaff* at the age of 80, and George Frederick Handel wrote the oratorio *Jephta* towards the end of his life whilst suffering from blindness, paralytic attacks and gout. Richard Strauss produced some of his most inspirational music – his *Four Last Songs* and *Metamorphosen*, an elegy for the Germany being destroyed in the bombing raids on Dresden, Berlin and other cities – in his last years. Another remarkable musician of a different kind is 90-year-old Fanny Waterman, the inspirational teacher and founder of one of the most prestigious piano events in the world, the Leeds Piano Competition. She is the living embodiment of the adage 'You don't stop working because you grow old; you grow old because you stop working.'

Contemporaries who would agree with this include the 88-year-old English painter Lucien Freud and the 91-year-old Austrian artist Maria Lasnig. I do not imagine that either of these are planning to retire soon. The French-born sculptor Louise Bourgeois (1911-2010) was working in her 100th year, and the French film director Eric Rohmer (1920-2010) was still making films in his late 80s.

In poetry – a quiet art – we find Robert Frost, Ezra Pound, Robert Graves and the indefatigable Kathleen Raine, all of whom were productive until the years of their deaths, as were the Irish playwright Samuel Beckett, the poet and Nobel Laureate Derek Walcott (aged 80) and the novelists P. D. James (aged 89) and Ruth Rendell (aged 79), all of whom are continuing to write at the peak of their form.

These are examples only known to me because of my interest in the arts, but there are of course many others – scientists, teachers, scholars and so forth – who have remained active in every field of human endeavour to the very end. There was the horticulturalist Collingwood Ingram, probably responsible for the introduction of most of the ornamental cherries in cultivation in Europe today; the Japanese pioneer of natural farming Masanobu Fukuoka; and the Norwegian climber and thinker Arne Naess, whose philosophy of deep ecology reflected his mystical reverence for mountains.

Other remarkable instances of creative activity at an advanced age include the Indian writer Rabindranath Tagore, the Jewish theologian Martin Buber, the German philosopher Martin Heidegger, the teacher Jiddu Krishnamurti, the interpreter of Zen Buddhism D. T. Suzuki, as well as one of the 20th century's greatest visual artists, the painter and sculptor Henri Matisse (1869-1954), who although a semi-invalid for the last 15 or so years of his life initiated a startlingly original creative medium: the coloured paper cut-out. The chief enterprise of his last years was another surprising choice: between 1948 and 1951 he designed and decorated a chapel in Vence for a convent of Dominican nuns.

No less contemptuous of the idea of retirement as a period of long, slow decline is perhaps the world's greatest singer, Placido Domingo, who at the age of 69 is delving into new operatic repertoire as a baritone. Why? "If you have a special ability, something that you can give people, you must make use of it and try to enrich other people's lives with it," he says.

Other remarkable men and women continuing to work as if age were of no consequence include the 82-year-old Russian activist Lyudmila M. Alexeyeva, who has been arrested for organising protests so many times in the last 43 years that she has become an expert at provoking and pestering the KGB. And, in an altogether different category, the world's oldest barber, Anthony Mancinelli, 98, who still cuts his own hair. "I am not even considering retirement because coming to work is what keeps me going," he says. Much the same could have been said by the 84-year-old naturalist and film-maker Sir David Attenborough, who has recently returned from three weeks in Antarctica where he was making a documentary about climate change.

Such people are, I know, very much the exception, but as such they are inspiring exemplars of the fact that, at least for some, life after retirement need not be experienced as a long, slow decline. For them there is still wisdom to be sought, work to be done and adventure to be had, not only physical adventure but spiritual also, the living adventure of the mind: the adventure that Matisse enjoyed with colour, the adventure with sound that Beethoven explored in his late string quartets, and the adventure of the inner spirit that Thomas Merton and others sought to plumb from within rather than from without. Is our life long enough to exhaust these kinds of possibility? To realise our human potential? To explore the special kind of excitement inherent in this search? To fulfil the nature of our particular gift? I doubt it! There remains a lot more to do.

When I was teaching art in a Yorkshire grammar school, I discovered the ubiquity of imaginative talent. Nearly every child was capable of producing visually exciting work, with only very few unable to give creative expression to their native abilities. It was an experience that taught me something about the unmined depths, the general hidden abilities in society, often extinguished in our late teens. But just as they say that the ground of Mongolia is packed with minerals, gold and oil, all waiting to be brought to the surface, so you are almost certainly packed with a potential that is also waiting to be discovered. You are very likely to be more talented than you think you are.

As a boy I remember pretending to be somebody I could never have become – Errol Flynn as Robin Hood – yet as an adolescent I was not aware of the obvious: that my fencing lacked athleticism, that I was too much of an introvert to become an actor, and even more obviously, that I was too young to grow a moustache! But was I alone in this kind of ignorance? I doubt it. How many others, I wonder, have been diverted from the natural course of their lives by attempting to become something that they were never meant to be. To live sincerely, declares Thoreau in *Walden*, is to "live deep and suck out all the marrow of life". How many of us are even trying to do that?

To do so requires a knowledge of who you are; it also needs a passionate single-minded commitment to realise your identity and a self-assurance that brooks no doubts. Yet all the while that we are being encouraged to consume, to emulate the lifestyle of the latest 'celebrity', to live more luxuriously than we have any need to do, we are probably ignoring the true scale of our native talent. Before it is too late, why not seek to emulate those whose temperaments have been richly fulfilled and have made something exceptional with their lives? It is highly probable that you will never become an Einstein, a Charlie Parker or a Marie Curie, but life is not a competitive race; what matters is the attempt to cultivate your seeds of talent, to realise that latent potential.

A truth which can only be whispered about the old is that we can be lazy and selfish. Many of us would appear to be content to do very little with our declining years, either because we view them as a time for well-earned recreation or are now too tired or ill to do anything significant with what remains. Another widespread and ingrained assumption is that we lack the talent to do anything of significance. But here as elsewhere, attitude is everything. Where did this belief originate? Did you discover it for yourself, or was it whispered in your ear by a teacher, a parent or a friend? Most probably it was our culture, or as D. H. Lawrence put it, "our accursed education" which taught you to doubt yourself. But now that you are old and have time on your hands, it is an opportunity to review that doubt. And if you feel you could be making more effective use of your time, then what is stopping you from doing so? Why have you so little confidence in yourself? Why do you lack the courage to stand out from the crowd? In spite of the fact that you may have developed some serious physical ailments, you are now free from the servitude of working for an income, and are largely free to do whatever you want.

Age provides the perfect opportunity to start exploring the possibilities of self-fulfilment. With luck on your side, it can be an enriching experience.

Chapter Six

THE GREAT UNCERTAINTY

Everything must be learned, from talking to dying.

Gustave Flaubert

To every thing there is a season, and a time to every purpose under the heaven:
A time to be born, and a time to die;
A time to plant, and a time to pluck up that which is planted;
A time to kill, and a time to heal; a time to break down, and a time to build up;
A time to weep, and a time to laugh; a time to mourn, and a time to dance . . .

Ecclesiastes, Chapter 3 verses 1-4

Oh threats of Hell and Hopes of Paradise!
One thing at least is certain – This Life flies;
One thing is certain and the rest is Lies;
The Flower that once is blown for ever dies.

Strange, is it not? that of the myriads who
Before us pass'd the Door of Darkness through,
Not one returns to tell us of the Road,
Which to discover we must travel too.

Edward Fitzgerald, *The Rubaiyat of Omar Khayyam*

EVERY TRADITIONAL CULTURE provides evidence of a preoccupation with an afterlife, each with its own tradition: a set of religious beliefs concerning the soul when it leaves the body and journeys to the next stage of life. For Tibetan Buddhists it is the monks who guide the souls of the dying through death to their next incarnation. For Christians, guardian angels are said to accompany the soul to Paradise. And in all cultures funeral rites, sometimes lavish, help survivors to come to terms with their loss.

Indeed, so universal is the assumption that something does happen after death that the reductionist scientific culture of the West is almost alone in its conviction that death is the end. A purely materialistic conception of birth and death was almost non-existent before our time. So is there life after death?

Sooner or later each one of us will confront this question: does the cessation of the body's various functions bring about a total end to life, a death not only of our physical functions but of our consciousness and soul? After our last breath has expired, might conscious existence continue in some form? In which case death might not be a conclusion but a continuation of the great journey of life. Or is our biological death the culmination of a short-lived consciousness, a sleep from which we can never hope to wake? "What dreams may come when we have shuffled off this mortal coil?" asks Hamlet anxiously. Does the spirit survive, bodiless, or is it reborn in a new human, animal or ancestor figure? Haunted by these doubts, we have long sought an answer to the question: is there life after death?

Together with a number of exceptionally capable and creative people who over the centuries have claimed direct experience of other dimensions of existence – Swedenborg, Blake, Jung and Rudolf Steiner come immediately to mind – countless millions of us – including Hindus, Christians, Muslims and members of all the indigenous tribes – have believed in the concept of an eternal soul, reincarnation and some kind of afterlife.

Peter and Elizabeth Fenwick's book *The Art of Dying* affirms that we are looked after throughout the transition from life to death by those who have loved us and returned to help us. A sensitive study of the near-death and out-of-body experience is also to be found in David Lorimer's *Survival? Body, Mind and Death in the Light of Psychic Experience*. I can also recommend Sogyal Rinpoche's *The Tibetan Book of Living and Dying* and *Gentle Dying: The Simple Guide to Achieving a Peaceful Death* by Felicity Warner. I have found these to be humane and eloquent guides to dying.

Perhaps even more comforting is the account of the death of the poet and painter, William Blake. Towards the end of his life, the poet lay in bed and, according to one observer, "began to sing Hallelujahs & songs of Joy & Triumph which Mrs. Blake described as being truly sublime in music & in verse". His first biographer, Alexander Gilchrist, continues the story of his death: "In that plain back room so dear to the memory of his friends, and to them beautiful from association with him – with his serene, cheerful converse, his high personal influence, so spiritual and rare – he lay chanting songs to melodies, both the inspiration of the moment, but no longer, as of old, to be noted down. To the pious songs followed, about six in the summer evening, a calm and painless withdrawal of breath; the exact moment almost unperceived by his wife who sat by his side. A humble female neighbour, her only other companion, said afterwards: 'I have been at the death, not of a man, but of a blessed angel!'"

This is certainly a comforting testament; but as a child of my time, I remain an agnostic about the idea of life after death. This is a view that flies in the face of the beliefs of many of my friends, but I cannot believe what I do not believe. And besides, they are themselves divided. One of them whose husband has recently died writes in confirmation of her belief in the certainty of a life after death. "It is an extraordinary encounter with reality but I am so glad that he died suddenly without illness and pain while he was still enjoying things – that makes it so much easier to bear, also that we had, over the years, explored together some of the antechambers of the spiritual realms. It was very clear to me when he died that he had shed an old suit of clothes (his body) that he no longer needed and freely flew into a different dimension. I am aware of him being around."

But almost in the same post comes a letter from another friend who, whilst thanking me for my letter of commiseration, makes it clear that her husband's death was not a beginning but an absolute end: complete extinction. So what is one to believe? How are we to comprehend the truth of this fundamental mystery? Perhaps we can only wait and see.

Meanwhile, I like to think that although the universe may not be a purposeless accident, I have no explanation of how or why or by what means it all began. There must be, one imagines, a deeper level of explanation, but what that is I do not know. What can we make of the fact that the American space Pioneer 10, launched in 1972, is already seven billion miles away from where I am writing these words? So just as I simply do not know how to consider these matters, nor do I know whether death is an end, a continuation, a passageway or, as some believe, a judgement.

In general I know that new life grows from the compost of that which has died. I also share the Buddha's view that theoretical intellectual exchanges are often little more than a waste of time and vital energy. So rather than spend time on fruitless metaphysical speculation about an unknowable future, in my view it is better to consider the more exacting if less exciting subject of how it is best to live one's present life.

There is relatively little guidance to be found within the many different faiths about what happens after death. Christians believe that at the end of the world Jesus will return to decide which of us deserves, on the one hand, to enjoy the bliss of union with God or, on the other, to suffer everlasting punishment in hell. In the cathedral of St Lazarus at Autun there is a depiction of this, the Last Judgement. A more famous rendering is to be found in Michelangelo's painting in the Sistine Chapel in the Vatican. In fact there are countless representations of this subject, including some surviving mediaeval Doom paintings in English churches, for example the one at Chaldon in Surrey.

According to Islamic belief there will also be a Day of Judgement, when we will be judged according to the way we have lived. After this Judgement each soul will experience one of two possible futures. The good will be rewarded by the existence of Paradise, a place of physical and spiritual pleasure with lofty mansions, gardens with rivers and trees full of fruits, and delicious food and drink. On the other hand the wicked will be punished, and far from feebly. Hell will include a fiery crater of various levels, the lowest of which contains a cauldron of boiling pitch. Belief in life after death (*al-akhirah*) is so crucial to the Islamic faith that any doubts about it would amount to the denial of Allah, whose word in the Qur'an is the foundation of its faith.

Other religions have differing ideas about what happens after death. Hindus believe that time, rather than being linear, is cyclical: humans do not live and die only once, but are reborn a number of times before reaching their final state, a process called reincarnation. Death for Hindus is not therefore a great calamity, not an end of consciousness, but a natural evolution of the human soul in the long journey of its life. The aim of the Hindu is to obtain freedom from this cycle of being born, dying and being reborn again and again.

The generally accepted Asian theory of reincarnation is also widely believed amongst those of the Buddhist faith. In its simplest terms, reincarnation is the theory that each human being lives more than one life. But there are other widely believed theories concerning life after death. There is transmigration of souls, the doctrine that a human soul passes after death into some other body, animal or human; and karma, the law of cause and effect or ethical causation which affirms that good or evil actions in your life determine your condition in lives to follow.

Death in a secular culture like our own is virtually a taboo subject, but one that fascinates nonetheless. Few of us have seen a dead person, let alone kept company with a dying one. Dying at home remains relatively rare, and medical science has done everything in its power to sanitise the entire experience. Although this is slowly changing, dying at home is as yet very far from commonplace.

Part of the reason is surely that most of us, and particularly those who live in cities, no longer understand our relationship to nature. It is assumed that we are separate from nature – after all, milk comes in plastic bottles, and very few people have ever visited an abattoir. The inevitable fact of death is hardly ever experienced as a natural part of life, but as something fearful to be avoided at all costs – don't bring the subject up, try to forget that it will ever happen to everyone you know, let alone to yourself. The overwhelming sense of powerlessness and bewilderment that strikes so many after a bereavement appears to colour the very subject of death, which can darken the thoughts of those still alive. Others, however, may face the prospect with a degree of equanimity, and even in some instances, when old age has become burdensome, with appreciation and even humour. Perhaps the wisest still regard it not only as a necessary conclusion but for the funeral to be a time for celebration as well as for grieving.

Coming to terms with death

Not only is it difficult to prepare the dying for death, but they (the dying) often fail to prepare themselves or their children. Yet, if for some reason you are unable to leave plans for your own funeral, at the very least you should have prepared a will, and specified in writing how you wish your body to be handled. Matters such as whether you would like to be buried or cremated, to die at home in a hospice or hospital, should not be left to those who survive you. I understand that some 70 per cent of people report that they would like to die at home, but in reality only 17 per cent actually do so.

It is however possible that the dying may have a more practical and philosophical view about it than we do. Sometimes it can be a compassionate thing to talk to the dying about death, but not always. Take your cue from them. It may be enough to be there and lightly hold their hands.

Dying

Michel de Montaigne expresses the fear of dying with his usual sanity. "If you don't know how to die, don't worry," he writes. "Nature will tell you what to do on the spot, fully and adequately. She will do this job perfectly for you; don't bother your head about it."

The funeral

Our ancestors treated their dead with love, fear, awe and respect, but rarely with the kind of embarrassed timidity which I have observed in some assembly-line funeral services in municipal crematoria. Some of those who have chosen a religious service may not have any belief, nor any idea of an alternative. They are simply cowed, perhaps, by the tragedy and solemnity of the event. How different from the rituals which used to accompany the dead in earlier civilisations, and even in Indian, Greek, Sicilian or Irish villages today.

Those who would like to get back in touch with a less wasteful, more personal way of dealing with death may choose burial in a natural setting. There is a growing interest in these Green, Natural and Woodland funerals, and the choice offered by the creation of alternative ceremonies. It is a choice best made in advance of the event.

No two funerals are the same. They vary in accordance with the age, the culture, and with the status of the deceased. Some are quiet, some joyful, some forgettable, others exuberant. For myself, I doubt if I have attended as many as a dozen of them over the years, although now that I am getting older I am called to more and more of them. Perhaps three or four have been memorable, unique experiences. In part, of course, they have been moving because of the friend who was being buried. But the location and design of the funeral, as well as the sincerity of the occasion, have also contributed to the experience.

I can remember the haunting beauty of the solo flute that accompanied the Plymouth-born social worker Mary Thomas to her grave; the triumphant singing of Bunyan's great poem, *To be a Pilgrim*, which concluded the funeral of my friend the painter Cecil Collins in London's Chelsea Old Church; and the quiet service of another friend, Dorothy Sherratt, in the church of the village of Goathland on the North Yorkshire Moors. (I still remember her husband's complete certainty that this was not the end; he and his wife would meet again, he told me, in the coming afterlife.)

But sadly, some of the funerals I have attended have been held in far less congenial environments: those heartless crematoria surrounded by beds of roses growing out of green pebbles.

Today, as Peter Levi writes, the greenness of the world is running out. The farewell to a dear friend is our last opportunity to renew it with grace. We must pray for the dead, and we must pray for ourselves.

The other day I attended the crowded funeral service of an elderly neighbour in an ancient village church. The man who had died had loved music, tradition and local history, and so these were strongly in evidence throughout the event. As we waited for the arrival of the coffin, carried by four sturdy but ageing undertakers, we listened to a Bach Chorale and recited the beautiful words of Psalms 39 and 90:

"Lord, thou hast been our refuge from one generation to another. Before the mountains were brought forth, or ever the earth and the world were made: thou art God from everlasting, and world without end."

"I know that my Redeemer liveth, and that he shall stand at the latter day upon the earth. And though after my skin worms destroy this body, yet in my flesh shall I see God: whom I shall see for myself, and mine eyes shall behold, and not another."

After the Committal, the congregation moved to the graveyard where the final resting place had been prepared. Here we remembered our lost friend, lowered our heads, admired the funeral flowers and threw a small handful of earth onto the coffin. Birds sang lustily.

I was reminded of other rural funerals: one for the poet and naturalist Teresa Whistler, who had lived in the village of Dolton most of her life; another for the potter Marilyn Hyde, who, after a service with songs from La Taizé, was buried in one of the loveliest churchyards I know – that of the Cornish poet and parson R. S. Hawker's Morwenstow, close to the Cornish cliffs and the sound of Atlantic breakers. Both funerals reflected the quiet sincerity of their lives. Both were accompanied by what is often called a 'eulogy', an address spoken by a friend or member of the family in praise of the deceased.

In contrast to these restrained and vernal occasions, accompanied as they were by the noble words of the service for the Burial of the Dead in the Book of Common Prayer, I remember the morning (the first of many) when I visited the famed cremation ground at Manikarnika Ghat on the riverfront at Varanasi in India. This was certainly something very different: an occasion of awesome power.

No city on earth is as synonymous with death as Varanasi. The old come here to die, sometimes thousands arriving every day. They bathe in the Ganges and pray to the rising sun. Here they wait for death in one of the city's many hospices that stand along the Ganges. I never spent an afternoon in the heart of the city without hearing the chanting of a funeral party on its way to the cremation grounds, where the body, wrapped in a golden sheet, is laid on a pile of wood before being burned. Manikarnika with its acrid smoky atmosphere and glowing red night sky, is as theatrically different from north Devon's vernal funerals as it is possible to imagine.

I understand that in Varanasi (Benares or Kashi as it is also called) mourning and wailing are thought to be bad luck for the dead; the atmosphere is one of almost casual solemnity in keeping with the belief that death in Kashi is to be counted a great blessing because it brings with it liberation from the earthly round of reincarnation.

Chapter Seven

THE ART OF AGEING

Beautiful young people are accidents of nature,
beautiful old people are works of art.

Eleanor Roosevelt

I T WAS OVER A YEAR AGO that I began to write this book. During
the ensuing months I have met many old people, read books on
the subject of age, lost several dear friends and noticed how the
skin of my hands has begun to wrinkle, which puts me in mind of
my long-dead father's.

So in this time, what conclusions have I reached about ageing?
Because there are many different kinds and rates of ageing, each
slightly different from the other, I'd judge that I've learned rather
less than might have been expected. Ageing is a spectre that
remains ominous but intangible. So much depends on circumstance: on wealth, health, attitude, ambition (or lack of it) and, of
course, one's genes. Only last week I was at the funeral of a
supremely talented person who to the last hour of his life – he died
aged 89 – had maintained high levels of interest and vitality. But
good fortune of this kind is now far from unique; we hear of more
and more people in their eighties and nineties who continue to
achieve remarkable things.

On the other hand, one of my oldest friends, poor soul, is
bedridden; suffering from an inoperable cancer, she can barely eat
and is virtually immobile. The worst of her pain is under control
but in reality she is living less than half a life; given the choice
between the humiliating indignities of her existence and a peaceful
end to it all, she would, she tells me, prefer to die.

So we have these extremes, a spectrum of possibilities ranging
from one of the most terrifying – a total loss of memory – to a

peaceful and sudden death. And in between there lies a wide variety of fates over which most of us have severely limited control.

Old age can take many forms: it can be peaceful; it can be horrific. If the latter, if you are unable to do all the things you would like to, if you are lonely, fearful of death, darkly depressed and sick in heart and body, there are still things you can do. But first you need to make every effort to come to terms with your unhappy condition: to accept it, albeit reluctantly but with stoicism. To rail against your plight, to fight your destiny, is fruitless and undignified. It has to be accepted. To do so may require an exceptional degree of fortitude, an unyielding stoicism, a defiant gallantry, a valour amounting to heroism, the heroism of those countless multitudes who suffer without complaint. I salute them, as I salute all those who suffer pain, indignity and loneliness with grace and courage.

The wonder of things

There is something else that you can do to ease the problems associated with advancing age; it is simple, universally applicable, cost-free and massively enjoyable: nothing more nor less than an undemonstrative appreciation of the wonder of things.

Just recently I have felt distressed, heavy and a trifle dejected – maybe it's simply that I'm getting older and my body is deteriorating, maybe it's something else? I don't know the cause, I don't know why I've felt this dispiritment. But then, just as mysteriously as this mood appeared, this very morning it simply lifted. At the time I was pulling back the bedroom curtains, temporarily blinded by the rising sun, I began to feel renewed: flooded with joy to be part of such a magnificent universe. Yes, the sunrise is a common-place event, but it's a miracle nonetheless. On any day, in any place, we live in a world surrounded and saturated by marvel: just this orchard with its apple trees in flower and the thick white crust of daisies covering the grass – a miracle; just the light on this patch of bare wall, or the cat sniffing at my face – both miracles; a baby's fingers holding tightly onto her blanket – yet another. Miracles everywhere! Miracles, commonplace, exquisite and deeply precious! Beauty is nature's free gift to us all, and the moments when it is experienced perhaps the most ecstatic of our lives.

Another of my suggestions to ease the melancholy of late age is anything but new – for it's an idea as old as the hills – a three-word maxim that has never been improved: *Count your blessings*. There is so much to be grateful for: the food we are receiving, the comfort we take for granted and the love we are receiving and giving to our friends. Confronted by the unknown, the unpredictable turns of our individual fates, love and simple lovingkindness, given and received, can provide us with the support we so sorely need at this most difficult of times.

"We do not receive wisdom," said Marcel Proust. "We must discover it for ourselves after a long journey that no one can take for us or spare us." That journey is none other than working to grow, love, explore, create and discover the miracle of life which, if only for a fugitive spell, awaits our appreciation.

I can only write from my own experience, which colours my life. If I'd lived a more difficult one, a life more shaped by misfortune and tragedy than the relative comfort and fulfilment I have enjoyed, I might now be writing something radically different – but I doubt it. For the gifted and ungifted, the fortunate and unfortunate alike, the ability to adapt, to learn and accept one's inborn limitations, to be in harmony with one's nature, is the determinant of all successful ageing. The American surgeon Sherwin B. Nuland observes: "Becoming what is known as elderly is simply entering another developmental phase of life. Like all others, it has its bodily changes, its deep concerns, its irremediable melancholy and its good reasons for hope and optimism. In other words it has its gains and it has its losses. The key word here is 'developmental'. Unlike most other animals, the human species lives long beyond its reproductive years, and continues to develop during its entire time of existence. We know this to be true of our middle age, a period of life that we consider a gift."

We should also recognise the value of the years that follow our allotted threescore years and ten. Living longer should allow us to continue the process of our development. It should give us more time to explore who we are: our identity, our destiny, the reason why we are alive. To enjoy our wonderful life-loving capacities. To celebrate the fact of being alive, and satisfy more of that all-important driving force of the good life: curiosity and some optimism.

Yet as we get older it becomes harder to maintain some of the things we have taken for granted: the spontaneity and energy of youth, to remember names, discover new friends and throw off a growing conservatism of attitude. It is also more difficult to be as energetic as we were. Paradoxically, some may feel more liberated, less constrained, and lighter, which may be the reason why some exceptionally creative people have produced their most revolutionary work at the end of their lives. Speaking for myself, I've also noticed a desire, even a craving, for the peace of a deep silence. Sometimes I'm happy enough to do nothing but sit and listen to the uninterrupted silence of my room. Old favourites are more profoundly enjoyed. As long as I can remember, I have loved the music of Handel, but never more so than I do today, when I am discovering aspects of it I never heard in the past. The same is true of my feelings for my friends: I appreciate them, and nature too, more than I ever did. The other day I espied a small patch of grassy earth, the sight of which gave me great pleasure. Before I had learned how to look, I doubt if I could have seen the full loveliness of those delicate spears of tender green, patterning the dark soil.

Walk cheerfully over the world

A friend has sent me a moving tribute to the author and critic John Gross, written by his son, Philip, winner of the T. S. Eliot Prize for Poetry in 2010. In a short but affectionate essay, entitled 'My Hero', he has described how his father lost his hearing.

"Birdsong went first," he writes. "Now there's mainly the confusing growl of traffic. Bang a car door and he'll startle, as if it's a gunshot. For him that isn't a figure of speech; 65 years ago he was ducking and weaving his way across Europe in the awful closing moments of the war.

"But that's another story, one he won't tell now, because words have deserted him – the three or four languages he had at his command gone with a series of small strokes.... Can you imagine, cut off from the sound of the human voice, and from your own voice? You can read just, inch by inch, up close, and your fine motor control isn't up to more than two or three words before it goes haywire.

"Now, look up. Address the world fairly in whatever phonemes you can muster. Put a bold foot forward. In the words of early Quaker George Fox, 'Walk cheerfully over the world.'

"We have never been a family for filial piety, still less for heroworship. I have no idea whether he was a brave man in that war, or simply human. But looking at my father now, the way he bears his old age... I call that a bit heroic."

Pierre Bonnard

In this context I will introduce the story of another person, not normally considered a hero, but for me he is one nonetheless. He is the painter Pierre Bonnard, who spent the duration of the Second World War holed up in his home, Villa du Bosquet, at Le Cannet in the south of France. His was a simple, unpretentious life, but towards its end one saddened by deep sorrow. The deaths of some of his closest friends, followed by that of his beloved wife, brought him loneliness and great sadness. He also suffered from the cold and shortages of petrol, food and coal. (Cartier Bresson's photographs, taken in the winter of 1944, show the old man's shivering figure wrapped in a coat to save fuel.)

For over a decade Bonnard had been painting some mystically beautiful pictures of his garden, culminating in the last of the series *L'Amandier en fleur* (The Almond Tree in Flower). By the end of the war, already bedridden and too weak to paint, he told his nephew Charles Terrasse to make some alterations. "The green on the patch of ground is wrong. What it needs is yellow . . ." A few days later (it was 23rd January 1947) Bonnard had died. He was 82.

Bearing in mind the sufferings of the war – of those in the concentration camps, the casualties of the battle for Berlin, of the bombing of Dresden and other German cities, the destruction of Hiroshima and Nagasaki, the terrible battle of Iwo Jima in the Pacific – the last years of Bonnard's life do not appear particularly dreadful. I am not suggesting that they were. But what inspires me, and what I'd describe as heroic in its own quiet, undemonstrative way, is that this desolate old man remained true to his vision of nature, and that his vision was a celebration of the glory and renewal of life.

L'Amandier en fleur is a painting of fecundity – an instinctive hymn to life, a song that exults the flush and fertility of nature.

Surrounded as he was by the pain and chaos of those terrible years, Bonnard was yet able to leave behind this token of his faith in the future of life on Earth! Celebration, not despair, was his final gift. Redemption, not realism, his ultimate message.

Love Your Life

Wondering how to bring this book to a conclusion, I have begun to see how the answer lies (as is so often the case) right under my nose. Until recently I had thought of Bonnard solely in terms of his art, but it occurs to me that the story of his life offers a great deal more – a liberating vision of the possibilities of a fulfilling old age – an age dedicated to giving back, returning, some of the wonder he had been given by the miracle of life. "However mean your life is," advises Thoreau, "meet it and live it; do not shun it and call it hard names. . . . Love your life, poor as it is." Vincent van Gogh observed, "The uglier, older, meaner, iller, poorer I get, the more I wish to take my revenge by doing brilliant colour, well arranged, resplendent."

Bonnard will be remembered as one of the greatest painters of the last century, but it is as an old man facing loneliness and adversity with courage, singleness of purpose and thanksgiving, that his importance for me now lies. I appreciate him as the model and touchstone for authentic human existence.

For the whole of the modern period, we have thought of the future in terms of the cultural property of the young. But it may be the old, those who have developed the art of living, whose wisdom has the most to offer us.

Chapter Eight

BRIEF LIVES

I would like to introduce you to a few people who, it seems to me, have made good and sometimes inspiring use of their lives. They are individuals who have explored and are exploring ways of finding fulfilment for themselves and of benefiting others, both known and unknown. All are models of creative courage – of how, as the poet Yeats described it, "soul can clap its hands" until the very end of life.

PETER ASHTON

"My wife and I have lived in the small mid-Welsh Border town of Montgomery for just over 50 years. Formerly the county town of Montgomeryshire, it nestles beneath the ruins of a thirteenth century castle from which the remains of the town's walls can still be traced. With a population of only a little over one thousand people, it retains its historic roots, with many half-timbered cottages, the fine Parish Church, and a Broad Street lined with Georgian houses.

"Because I came as a GP, we were fortunate to be immediately involved with the community, and at one time knew nearly everyone in the town and the surrounding farms. Retirement has enabled me to continue a friendship with my former patients. Jean and I are privileged to know and enjoy the company of many delightful older people as well as younger friends. Our four children have given us twelve grandchildren, and we have a family which gives us much happiness (and sometimes a little heartache!).

"Age? I'm now 79 but can barely believe it. Advice? Yes, it's quite simple: savour the moment. Consciously develop an awareness of the present. Looking ahead can fill one with foreboding; looking backwards can fill one with regrets. My advice is that we should just take time to be, to enjoy living. To keep an active interest in life.

"I believe ageing is about attitude, the willingness to adapt, to think creatively, to live positively and be actively interested in other people. I struggle to achieve these aims, and difficult as they are, every day provides us with fresh opportunities to learn something new.

"My Christian faith is central to everything else. I believe that this life is held within an everlasting love which we experience and accept in faith. There may be rare moments when I can glimpse that truth, perhaps seen through beauty and love, times when heaven and earth touch each other, when sadness and joy strangely merge. I believe that the peace and reality of those moments are a preparation for the time when we move on from this life.

"I am closely involved with the local churches, and after retirement joined the Acorn Christian Healing Foundation, an organisation designed to promote understanding of Christian healing. I also set up a local group called CADFAN designed to bring churchgoers and those working in medical care together. From time to time I lead services.

"In addition I am involved in plans to create a Care Home in the town, and after many years our plans are nearing completion. It is our intention that it will be integrated into the community, providing a venue for a computer club, and a place where older people can meet and share meals.

"We have so much for which to be thankful."

BARBARA BLACKMAN

"I have to admit that my driving force is Curiosity."

I met Barbara Blackman, now aged 81, on a visit to Sydney in 1988. She had worked as a librettist, child psychologist, artists' model, magazine columnist, radio producer for Radio for the Print Handicapped and as an oral historian for the Australian National Library. She was a member of the C. G. Jung Society and the National Federation of Blind Citizens. Her pleasures were contemporary music, coffee drinking, visiting Perth, solitude and her three offspring and six grandchildren. Because of the difficulties of interviewing someone living at that distance, Barbara wrote the following account of her life.

"My mother, who lived to be 96, wrote to me at 90 from a Retirement Village: 'Live as long as you can. Sort yourself out, and your belongings.' Wise mother, obedient daughter.

"My friend Ella Ebery is turning 90 and still running a country newspaper, as she has done for the last 50 years, though she has now given up running the local Dramatic Society. Ever since she turned 80, she has been periodically 'discovered' by the media in print or screen form. Now she uses the discovered media to protest about octogenarian drivers in her back-blocks country town losing their licences for driving too slowly or parking crookedly. A couple of Christmases ago I sent her a card. In my exuberance I said: 'Ain't old age wonderful!' She wrote back: 'No. It hurts.'

"Seven years ago I came to live in Canberra, the bush capital of Australia and its best-kept secret. A city of less than 350,000 people, it has four universities and the National Gallery, Museum, Library, War Museum, National Archive, Film and Sound Institute, many U3A (University of the Third Age) classes, Choral Groups — and kangaroos beside the Lake and often in the streets.

"Its elder population is vigorous, with people in retirement from academic, diplomatic, medical and other professions, and farms close enough to go home at night. I call my house in sight of the Lake *Sisu* — a Finnish word meaning 'endurance energy' or 'energy for endurance' — a good place for living out my last lap in an intimacy with all that I love in Nature and Culture. Such friends I have made, such events attended, such speeches and concerts I have heard, such picnics. I remember an old painter I interviewed in my Oral History days, John Saltry, whose career went back to the 'black-and-white' press artists of the thirties; he said at the end, 'My life has been one long picnic. There have been some dark and rainy days, but I have found shelter. I am grateful to Whomsoever invited me.'

"I have had two marriages, one for 30 years (to the celebrated Australian painter Charles Blackman), one for 20, and two affairs, one before and one between. Four times I blew the whistle, peeled off my skin and grew another. I am still a friend of all four, still part of loving embrace whenever we meet. Love implants itself in the other, an osmosis that outlasts change. . . .

"Brought up Biblical, with a taste for traditions, I have always held that at threescore years and ten one should be all packed up and ready to go. Not that one has to go, one is always invited to stay on longer. One has to be prepared for that encore. Perhaps that is what my mother meant by calling old age the Promised Land, explaining that, when one's life's work is done, then the present is not carrying the weight of the future. The work well done, the future will take care of itself. Canberra is the scene of my Promised Land. I was three years overdue in getting here. Those three last years of my worldly work were difficult. I had to move a mountain.

"Something about coming to Australia's capital aroused the citizen in me, the wish to give back whence I had been so bountifully given. The great paintings that had come to me I gave to public galleries, and the surplus monies I had been encumbered with I channelled off to orchestras and a lecture foundation. This is the joy of long living. One can see one's offloading helping to make the world go round. *Sisu* is just the right size for me, with open space which makes it seem bigger, a surround of narrow garden that makes it feel part of the green and flowering land, expansive enough for parties large and small, a guest room mostly occupied, an upstairs light and sunny room in which to write, and the best of loudspeakers to make the music loud and clear. The theme of my last life, 'Hospitality, Contemplation, Study', still holds place.

"Nor have I dragged along with me a whole museum of past furniture. I see some long-loved pieces when I visit houses of younger friends. Harmony in my furnishing comes from the company of beloved fellow travellers – the long narrow settee in which, as an infant, I remember my father lying horizontal in his last illness, the plaited cane chair in which my mother suckled me, the all-purpose table pounded with argument and anecdote, spilt upon by wine and casseroles; the Jacobean chest of drawers picked up cheap in a Camden Town street market, chairs that were in my first published book of essays – *Certain Chairs* of 1968 – and walls thick with paintings from my first husband, and those of others I have acquired. I am happy. Happy things happen here.

"My house, like myself, has a secret chamber. Built for a garage, but I have made it an archive room. I have kept my papers as I have kept my memories. Here are boxes of documents, letters, cuttings and manuscripts from my other lives over the years, all in course of sorting for posterity, whomsoever that might be. Within myself there are the secret chambers of the sorrows I have become accustomed to bear: the sorrow of the missing father, the sorrow of the blindness that grew from childhood and has been complete for more than half my life, and the sorrow of grandchildren being inaccessible because of parents' distance or busyness.

"These sorrows have sowed splendours that might otherwise have been unknown. I have some grand elders who have fathered me with their company and wisdom. I have lived in a 'different country' among pleasures from which sight-addicted people are veiled, where radio and audio books have pleasure and have informed me. Silence and solitude are immeasurable gardens beyond the Green Door. Other little children have grown up as my friends with all the cuddles, stories, secrets, jokes, adventures shared, so that 'Nanna' is as warm a name to me as any form of 'grandmother'.

"In old age we are indeed explorers, My mentor, sternest critic and most loving kin, was a wise old woman I did not meet until she was 70 (although she was my father's cousin), which allowed us just on 30 years of wonderful friendship. She used to say that she had enjoyed this earthly life so well that she was sure death would be a most interesting experience. She went to her death like a bride to the altar in her 100th year, and has left me buoyed with hope and, like Samuel Beckett's *Malone* (who takes a whole book dying), intending to live alive until the last breath, no matter how. And she did."

EMMA BROFFERIO

The ancient hill town of Gubbio in Umbria, sombre and stony, is the home of the Marchese Emma Brofferio, 97 years of age. She now lives in one room, the gatehouse of her old home, a narrow, simply furnished apartment close to the centre of the town where until recently she used to do her own shopping. Nowadays she relies on two local women, one nearly 70, who give her a helping hand.

"I like a variety of occupations," she tells me. "I read, I crochet, I translate from Italian into English and vice versa, but to a large extent I look after myself. I like living on my own; I don't want anyone living with me. I've got everything I want and I have so much to do – and I'm so much slower than I used to be – but I am never lonely." I doubt if this indomitable but sprightly old woman knows the meaning of boredom.

"I've had a good life, and have what a lot of people don't possess – friends, relatives, enough money, and all the little comforts anyone could desire." Her memory is excellent, her vitality unbounded, her charm infectious.

This independence of spirit is characteristic of a woman, Italian by birth, who has lived a full life in India and England as well as Italy, had two husbands and three children but is now content to live by herself in a slip of a room characterised by silence and simplicity. Emma Brofferio regards old age as a time to devote to prayer. She is a Franciscan Tertiary, that is one who has chosen to live in the world as their forerunners did at the time of St Francis, and to do so as simply as possible as a witness to Christ in her daily life of prayer and sacrifice. She attends church once a week and spoke movingly of her prayers for a granddaughter who, only the day before we met, had undergone a major operation. "The Church is good enough for me. Love God and your neighbour, that's good enough for me." I wonder if there is anything more that she'd like from life? "Yes, serenity of spirit," she answers with decision.

"So long as one is alive, we should be making use of our talents. Do something, whatever it is. Keep going. But seek to make the best of what you have been given and live according to what you believe is right. And as far as daily living is concerned, it's important to safeguard your health. Be disciplined and be true to yourself." Then she quoted something by Dante about a tower which withstands the wind and stays absolutely still in spite of its buffeting. The moral of this is that we should stand upright and never be swayed by passing circumstance and external pressure.

"The world is in a very sad state. People don't seem to realise that money simply cannot provide them with any depth of satisfaction. Wealth and success are all very well; but once we have them their allure just fades." I asked her whether she was looking forward to being 100. "No, I don't want to live to be 100." This woman knows her own mind.

MARY CUZNER

Approaching the neatly gardened bungaloid estate at Westward Ho! where my wife's parents used to live, I catch the sound of Mary's joyful humming as she washes dishes at the sink. She exudes ebullience, a contagious happiness. Nursing has been her career, helping others her fulfilment.

Now 90 years of age, Mary is a woman of exceptional, if extrovert, energy. She is 'fighting fit', as they say. She relishes reading, knitting ("I've made thousands of cardigans and pullovers"), cooking, crossword puzzles, travelling, visiting the theatre, gardening on a regular basis, and at times a tot or two of whisky. Driving? "Oh yes, definitely." And until three or four years ago, she was also surfing. "Now that I'm retired," she says, "there is more time to be quiet, to think, to pray and listen to music – especially Mozart and Beethoven – but people are the real centre of my life. I am fond, very fond, of people."

Its taproot is her Catholic faith from which she draws deep nourishment. "I go to Mass every day and say the rosary. Faith has provided me with the Way, the Truth and the Life, and although from time to time I have experienced a few doubts, I have never seriously questioned my belief. It has provided me with the right answers and will do so until the end. My motto in life, John, is a simple one: always be merry and bright. I don't sit back waiting for the Great Reaper for I enjoy life to the full and greet every day with optimism. Yes, believe me, I am truly grateful to be alive. I really enjoy being alive.

"Both my mother and three of my aunts were nurses and I've followed in their footsteps all my life – it started in 1936 when I trained as an orthopaedic nurse, then on to St Bartholomew's Hospital for general training, for midwifery; then on to Plymouth for Queen's Nurses training, then on to four more years district nursing and more midwifery in Tavistock; then health training in Battersea and 20 years in charge of North Devon where I am still living. Oh, yes . . . in the fifties I also enjoyed five wonderful years in Malta. I would have liked to marry, but I never met anyone who really captured my imagination as nursing did. If the Good Lord took me tomorrow I could say that I've enjoyed a wonderfully good life – and I really mean it, too.

"Yes, I know that I am getting older. I don't feel old, but there you are. We can only do what we can in the time we have been given. I'm slower than I used to be, but I like to believe that I now have a greater understanding of people's problems than in the past.

"'Keep right on to the end of the road'. Our death is inevitable but it's only the beginning of all the rest. And believe me, there's a lot more to come!"

MARIANNE DE TREY

Marianne de Trey CBE, aged 96, lives by herself in a one-storey wooden house tucked away in a peaceful quarry in the village of Dartington in south Devon. Adjacent to this sylvan property, originally built and lived in by the patriarch of the British Craft movement, Bernard Leach, Marianne has had her own workshop for the last 50 years.

The Cabin is a simple building, modestly furnished with some beautiful 17th-century furniture, a small collection of books on pottery, religion and philosophy, and in a prominent position over the fireplace a vigorous watercolour by her late husband, the potter and painter, Sam Haile, killed in a road accident in his 39th year. Undeterred by this disaster and by the pottery's destruction by fire in 1957, Marianne, an especially independent person, has never looked back.

Born in 1913 of Swiss parents, she has now outlived the small group of illustrious potters distinguished by age no less than by the quality of their work: Lucie Rie who lived until the age of 93, Bernard Leach who lived until he was 92, Shoji Hamada, who lived until the age of 84, and Michael Cardew who died at the age of 82. In recognition of her singular contribution to the craft of pottery, Marianne was awarded a CBE in 2006. Our conversation was strongly characterised by her natural optimism.

"I have always been lucky," she tells me, "always capable of dealing with difficulties when and however they arise. Yes, I'm slower now than in my youth and my handwriting has become very small, but never mind, life continues to be exciting; there is always something new to try, something new to discover. Each clay is different, each kiln and each fuel and glaze composition is so highly complex that the potentiality for experiment is endless. There's always a better pot to be made, but sadly, now that I am old and physically less able, I have doubts that I shall make it. But how lucky I have been to spend so many years just doing what I enjoy in the company of such enthusiastic and dedicated students and apprentices! Yes, there is always something new to try.

"I am sorry for those people who haven't anything to do – or so they think! Nearly all of us possess the five senses and they should certainly be used. My mother taught me to go round our garden and learn about plants. My father taught me how to make an effort and to stretch myself. Today, I'm afraid I can't do much gardening – getting up from kneeling down is difficult – but I do all my own cooking and have some really wonderful friends. No, I can't any longer bath myself, and can find myself asleep in my chair, but not to worry – I'm still enjoying it all so much, so much. Yes, I do get depressed by the news and all the crises, but I am an optimist about the future. Life is simply so exciting. I am an agnostic about the possibilities of a life after death, but then the future doesn't really worry me that much. Just let's make the most of what we have been given. That's a lot, you know."

GERTRUD
HUNZIKER-FROMM

Gertrud Hunziker-Fromm, aged 94, lives on a wooded hill in a quiet district of Zurich. After wandering through her beautiful garden, she leads us to a table laid with silver utensils, delicate plates and a delicious cherry cake.

She is a practising psychoanalyst who has lived with her companion Ursula Kunz since her husband, the painter Max Hunziker, died almost 30 years ago. She was a cousin of the psychoanalyst and social critic Erich Fromm, and of the art historian Ernst Gombrich.

She speaks slowly, like a philosopher.

"I feel at times both old and young. For a long time I've ceased to make plans and, as you see, I can no longer move as quickly as I once did and would like to be able to do once more. But I accept that being slow is part of ageing. There are advantages in becoming old. I now live more in the moment than I once did. When you are young you also live in the moment, but I believe that you are probably less aware of it. You appreciate the beauties (and I mean beauties) more as you get older; there is the oleander, the abelia, all the flowers here. Wonderful. As to my memory, that is up and down. It's good for the things that interest me and poor for the things which do not – like taxes!

"Yes, at different times I feel a variety of ages too. But especially young when I listen to Schubert. I grew up in a family where quartets were played once a week – so I know them well. Yet however many times I have heard one of his quartets – or the octet – I often feel that I am listening to the music for the first time.

"As to the matter of a life after death, well, I simply do not know. It must remain an open question, a mystery like so many other things. Some people – but I am not one of them – have complete certainty about everything, but quite simply I have never met their God on his throne above the clouds. Why do I like cats? I really can't say either!

"I get much less upset nowadays than I did in the past. It no longer bothers me if I am or am not accepted. I don't take people's opinion of me seriously. Love is the only energy in this world which does not need an explanation.

"Old age, if you are open to it, if you accept it, is a wonderful period of your life.

"What do I most enjoy? So many things. I love to be in my garden, I love to be in the meadows, the mountains, to listen to good music, to look at good paintings, to read good books. I am currently reading Meister Eckhart, the seventeenth-century German mystic poet Angelus Silesius, and St John of the Cross. I would so much have liked to have met the poet Regina Ullmann. There is so much to learn and enjoy."

Before we left, Gert Hunziker took us to see her late husband's studio. It is a large and silent room full of his dramatically powerful paintings that await, like Sleeping Beauty, the kiss of public recognition.

DICK JOY

"Were it not that I am passionately fond of the contours of my country, I should not be here." – Paul Cézanne

Dick Joy is an affable, unpretentious, firm-minded elder who since the age of three has lived in the village of Landkey (population 2,400) to the south-east of Barnstaple in Devon. I describe him as an elder not only on account of his age – he is 83 – but because he is quite definitely 'a senior member of a tribe who has authority'.

After the death of his wife five years ago Dick Joy has lived alone. He cooks for himself, tends a substantial vegetable allotment and used to keep a Jersey cow, some sheep and poultry – but no longer. Nowadays he has some difficulty in walking, and it's obvious that he has lost much of the physical vigour of his earlier years. Yet at heart he remains unchanged. He is the kind of countryman that I've been fortunate to have known for decades; the kind celebrated in the work of H. G. Massingham, George Sturt and my friend the American poet and social critic, Wendell Berry – that is to say the kind whose attention, memory and affection for village people has not been alienated from the land.

It is not for nothing then that he is known as Mr Landkey. For more than 50 years he has served on Landkey's Parish Council, many of them as chairman. For 40 years he was on the Village Hall Committee, and he has been involved with the United Charities and Horticultural Society, of which he is the current President. You name it, and he has contributed his bit – the impulse stemming, it seems, not only from a deep affinity and attachment to his native village, but from a sense of responsibility towards those who had voted for him. Listening to this octogenarian, who as a young man had opened his heart and mind to the teachings of socialism, I saw the highest example of a predisposition towards social fairness and equality.

During the course of our conversation he was keen to show me the results of the elections in which he had sought to become a Parish Councillor: in every case he had won by a thumping majority. His services to the community at large had been recognised when he had been made a Justice of the Peace, and in 1999 was awarded an MBE. For his first interview for a job, he said, he wore a bib and braces, but at the Palace he had worn a dark suit.

Dick Joy entered the village school at the age of three and left at 13. In those days, you spoke when you were spoken to and rose from the table only after permission had been granted. Believing that discipline matters in all things, and perhaps most of all in work, he has never doubted the value of obedience and careful time-keeping. In his early teens he worked with horses on a local farm, but then took up an apprenticeship as a carpenter at the Mill Road Depot in Barnstaple. At the age of 23, a year before the Lynmouth flood disaster, he was taken on by the County Council's Roads Department. A tragedy for many, the flood was to give him an exceptional experience of bridging and road construction. Ten years later he was appointed Foreman of a team responsible for the maintenance of the roads across Exmoor, a job he retained until he took early retirement in 1981.

Listening to the account of his life, I was struck that although the road works had sometimes been carried out under the most trying circumstances, in all weathers and when his team were physically exhausted, Dick Joy spoke of them without a trace of rancour. He had done what had to be and done it to the best of his ability – clearing, for example, an obstructed road to allow a woman in labour to reach the hospital with as much speed as possible. It is not every day of the week that one meets someone who has had to deal with snow on Exmoor.

The famous winter of 1962-3 is a case in point. Mid-November saw a belt of snow almost stationary on Exmoor. Then after Boxing Day it lay at least 12 inches deep over the area. The main fall, however, did not arrive until the end of January. In Somerset 160 villages were cut off; 20-foot snow-drifts were common, and up to 30 feet of snow was found in places. Excavation machinery was brought in from all over England, but snow-ploughs got stuck or broke down, and as soon as roads were cleared snow drifted over them again. The Army was brought in and RAF helicopters were in constant use, delivering food and medicine for people and animals, and taking the ill and injured to hospital.

1978 saw another terrible winter, but even at the best of times the moor can be treacherous. Yet Dick Joy and his team maintained their work through every kind of hardship.

After our talk we visited a field in the middle of the village in which about 60 Mazzard trees had been planted. Landkey has long been famous for this sweet cherry; there is a record of its sale in Barnstaple market in the 15th century, but in recent years the fruit has all but disappeared as a commercial crop. Until the 1950s every farm had its orchard. But in the last 40 or so years the number of orchards in Britain has declined by two thirds – around 150,000 acres have been lost. In Devon alone, almost 90 per cent of orchards have disappeared since 1965. It may be thought that in the grand scheme of things this is a loss which hardly matters, but I believe it does. Whenever a local culture is diminished, whenever the diversity and richness of a town or landscape is destroyed, we are all the losers. I imagine that Dick Joy, with his fierce commitment to everything native to his forbears and to Landkey, must have felt something of this kind. At all events, he was able to persuade the Parish Council to take the step which rescued the Mazzard from almost certain oblivion. It secured a £35,000 grant which enabled the orchard of these cherries to be planted. All four species of Mazzard – Greenstem Black, Black Bottler, Dun Small Black and Hannaford – were saved and are currently thriving.

Whilst we were visiting the site, Dick Joy pointed out another field which he had managed to rescue from inappropriate development. Its grass, glossy in the morning's powerful wind, was a wonderful sight. "I see it as my duty to act as a custodian of the countryside and to leave it in a better condition than when I came here." "Have you lived a fulfilled life?", I asked him. He hesitated to answer, but told me that he hoped so and emphasised the importance of living close to nature.

Looking up Landkey in W. G. Hoskins' wonderful book on Devon, I saw that his description of the county as the "immemorial, provincial England, stable, rooted deep in the soil, unmoving, contented, and sane" might also be the perfect description of people such as Dick Joy.

SATISH KUMAR

The youngest person in this group of biographies, Satish Kumar (born 1936 in Rajasthan, India), has been included not so much because of the considerable range of his activities – writing, lecturing, travelling and editing Resurgence *magazine – but because his background is radically different from that of all the other contributors, many of whom come from a tradition fundamentally influenced by a monotheistic religion such as Judaism and Christianity.*

Today, as well as editing Resurgence *he is a Visiting Fellow of Schumacher College in Dartington, which he helped to found in 1991. He lives in north Devon with his wife June.*

"At the age of nine I became a Jain monk, and as monks we were always required to think about the cycle of birth and death: the idea is that through the practice of penance, fasting, meditation, walking and teaching – all these activities help to free you, to liberate you, from bondage (which is called Karma). And when you are free, your death becomes 'moksha', which is the ultimate liberation. That is a kind of immortality of the soul, rather than the body. So you are free from the body and your soul is immortal.

"It is a faith – a faith based on the teachings and experiences of the enlightened beings – and when you experience it you are liberated, you are no more back in the world. I cannot say that I myself experienced it, but I believed it in terms of having a faith. So during that time I was required to pray that I might live and die in a pure state of mind, one free of bondage, free of attachments – and that means bondage from fear, anger, greed, pride. So I pray to die in that state of mind. Death is not to be feared, but to be welcomed. Death is absolute, essential, necessary, an integral part of life; if there is no death, then you are stuck in bondage and in your body. So only through death can you liberate your self, your soul from the body.

"However, during that life, whether you have illness or health, whether something positive or negative is happening, you should treat it with equanimity. Do not get exuberant when you get something positive or gain something, and do not get depressed when you lose something. That is the idea.

"I am sustained by that because that is the groundwork that took place in my childhood and has remained throughout my life, so I have never experienced any anxiety about death or fear of death. I have not felt fear of old age. I don't feel 'Oh! what will happen when I am old, when I die – will it be painful, will it be difficult?', etc., etc. The teachings of the Jain tradition I received in my childhood have sustained me. So even now when I am 74, I have no fear of death – I positively welcome it. Whenever I shall die, I will be ready.

"As long as you have a body you have pain. In the same way, as long as you have a human life there is sorrow. Like physical pain, there is also mental and psychological sorrow and sadness. So I know that will be there: I can't completely escape from that human condition. However, beyond that I have a state of mind where I believe that I can practise equanimity. When there is a birth of a child there is joy – I have just had the birth of a grandchild. There is joy, but I try to treat it with equanimity. Birth and death are part of life. Don't get too excited when there is a birth, and don't get too despondent when there is a death.

"My father died when I was four years old, and that is the first memory of my life. I have a very vivid memory of him lying in state, and of my family in very great deep sorrow: my mother crying, my sisters crying, and my sisters-in-law crying, my brothers crying and the family very much suffering. So in a way there was a kind of paradox, a contradiction. On the one hand we were all Jains, who had been taught to treat loss and gain with equanimity, but on the other hand as humans we could not escape from our emotions.

"And that, in a way, unsettled me, even at the age of four, and ever since then I was in search of finding the answer to death. My mother used to go to see the monks, and so I went with her and one day I told the monks that my father had died and everyone was very sad in our family, and I asked whether there was any way to overcome death. And my teachers, the Jain monks, told me this idea, this theory that the only way to be free of birth and death is to renounce the world, and live a pure life of minimum action, minimum attachment and eventually complete non-attachment. And that the best way to live a life of detachment and purity is to leave home and leave the world and become a monk. So I became a Jain monk at the age of nine.

"The other thing I experienced in my very young life was that there was a monk called Kundan who was over 70, and one day he decided that since he was becoming frail and no longer able to do various things, he would fast until his death. I was with Kundan, and I was very intrigued and impressed. This is a Jain tradition, where many people, particularly nuns and monks, but many laypeople as well, embrace death. And my own mother, when she was 80, she felt the same as Kundan – that now I am too frail and it's time to go. So one morning she went walking to see her daughters, friends and family to say goodbye, to say that from tomorrow she was going to fast to death. In a way that was quite shocking, but on the other hand because we have that tradition we know that this is how some pious, religious and spiritually oriented people go, how they die. So my mother was seen as a courageous brave person. One day she declared: 'Tomorrow I will face death and will start to die and not eat anything.' The news spread among friends and family and among well-wishers, and even among the Jain community at large. The next 35 days were a great celebration of her life, and her work and her creativity.

"In India we say that if you live well, you die well. So your focus and your thoughts should have two sides. One side is not to worry about death: if you live well today, death will be fine. The other side is that you should be ready to die at any time. Be prepared, be ready. We were always told to keep our suitcase packed and be ready. You don't know when you will die, so be ready and act as if you may die tomorrow. Always remain light and detached and without too much burden on your shoulders.

"If your mind is prepared with equanimity, then you know that being in good health and being ill are natural conditions of the body. And therefore if you become ill, it will pass. Health will follow illness, and illness will follow health. And if it doesn't pass, then you will go, you will die, and that will be liberation for this body. In the Hindu tradition, soul does not die, only the body dies. Soul, like space, is eternal – only the house that is built will fall. Some houses might stand for 20, 30, 50, 500 years, but in the end they all fall. And civilisations fall, the cities fall, the big trees – some last 500 years – but in the end they die. So this is the eternal truth of existence, that change and birth and death and beginning and end are all part of life.

"So neither mourn death nor be exuberant. What is the opposite of mourning? Celebration is wonderful, but don't get too excited with birth and don't get too despondent with death. Celebrate rain and sunshine. Celebrate night and day. Celebrate everything. Whatever is happening is the beauty and the mystery of existence, so celebrate the beauty and mystery of existence, which involves everything. There is no single factor, it's a diversity, so celebrate everything."

JAMES LOVELOCK

James Lovelock, aged 91, is an independent scientist, inventor and author, who works from his home-cum-research station in Devon. He lives with his second wife, Sandy, surrounded by 35 acres of trees which he has planted.

His achievements include the invention of an instrument crucial for documenting the use of the pesticides like DDT and ozone-destroying chlorofluorocarbons. In the early 1950s, while working on a device to re-animate frozen animals, he also came across an idea which led to the invention of the microwave oven. But more importantly he also introduced the idea of Gaia, a theory which proposes that the planet behaves as if it were a single living organism, constantly adapting to the needs of the life forms it supports.

In recent years he has written seven books about Gaia as well as an autobiography 'Homage to Gaia', and most recently 'The Vanishing Face of Gaia'.

"I never thought I'd have a long life. At 50 I was overweight and smoked around 10 cigarettes a day, and suddenly I found that I couldn't walk more than 100 yards without severe angina, a crushing pain in my chest. I knew the books said it was serious, and that relatives should be told that in all probability I'd only another six months to live. So I thought, 'To hell with this!' After a month of taking it easy and sitting around I decided that I was never going to get better, so I looked at the 300-foot hill above the village of Bowerchalke in Dorset where we were then living, and thought 'I'm damn well going to climb it' – and I did! After three months of working at it, I had recovered. I'd built up a whole series of arteries that helped my heart. That option is open to everyone. If you sit back and feel sorry for yourself, you'll die.

"Of course, it can be hard work, but there can be tremendous awards. Within two years I was climbing mountains in Ireland. We had a monitoring station on the slopes of Hungary Hill on the Beara peninsula, and I used to go up it most days; it had the cleanest air in Europe and it's a wonderful part of the world.

"Today, I'm just surprised at my age! There was a wise doctor we had at Holsworthy, and in my eighties I went through a very bad phase with endless operations. So I asked this doctor, "How long have I got?" He said, "Forget about it! Always remember that if you're relatively fit and there's no immediate threat to life, you have three more years." And for me that was wonderful news, because that amount of time is quite enough. Whether you're nine or 90 it's the same thing. If you're fit you'll be around for three more years. It's a wonderful thought. It stops you worrying.

"Just now I'm playing with the idea of writing another book, and the promised flight to space in a rocket is still on. After December 7th (2009) there will be a test flight, and the Federal Aviation Authority, the body that decides if it's safe for flight, will say yes or no, or if modifications are required. The vehicle is planned to go high enough to see the Earth and to be up in space for five minutes or so. Of course this has a special excitement and piquancy for me because the whole idea of Gaia came when I was considering the Earth as seen from space and wondering how it was that the Earth had remained over thousands of millions of years so remarkably accommodating. I wouldn't miss this flight for anything. The exciting and dangerous part is coming back, re-entering the atmosphere. It glides like the shuttle and has got to land at the right airport. But I've faith in Sir Richard Branson!

"Turning to the question of health, the most important single activity for me at least has been the value of a vigorous walk to make my heart work hard. Doing it three times a week has a spiritual as well as a physical effect. But, if you want to know, I am far from happy about people living longer than the average life span. From a personal point of view it's understandable, but from the point of view of the health of the planet, it's deplorable. I want to write about this dichotomy in my next book.

"Of course, I have been accused in the past of all kinds of New-Agey-sounding nonsense, inviting forgivable scepticism, but I do believe that if we fail to put the planet's welfare at the heart of our plans, the result will be a disaster. The Earth is already disabled by the insidious poison of greenhouse gases, and much worse can yet come – ice caps melting, the oceans rising and the world's cities at sea level – London, New York, Tokyo – disappearing under the waves at some as yet unknown future date.

"On Gaia's side I can see we almost need a new kind of religion to replace the present human-centred one. The new faith would put the Earth as the centrepiece for everything. But there are problems with religions, not least because they are human and divide into sects and tribes.

"It seems to me that we are not yet clever enough to handle the planet. It's my speculation that things are going to get very rough, but nobody really knows when that's likely to be. All that you can say is that putting the amount of CO_2 into the atmosphere which we are now doing, coupled with taking away land for farming to feed people all over the world, is almost certain to be harmful. If we continue, at some time or other the planet will move to its next stable state, one which it has been in many times in the past – we have records of that – a state about 5° or 6° hotter than it is now. But once it reaches there, at least it won't go any hotter – Gaia works – and it will stabilise. . . . If it were to get any hotter, then we'd all die. It'll work, it'll be damn uncomfortable and it is going to take at least 100,000 years before it cools down.

"When I was a boy, old people were an important part of society; they were thought to possess wisdom, and to them people turned for comfort and serenity. But I'm sorry to say that this is no longer the case. What I've discovered is that you don't seem to know you are growing old. You don't feel any different from how you felt in the past. I feel today just about the same as I did 30 or 40 years ago.

"I can also say that how you age seems to be largely to do with your genetic inheritance. In some ways life can be said to resemble a game of poker, where even when you have been served a really bad hand, it can with determination and ingenuity, to some extent at least, be turned round. To be born with a serious physical disability like blindness is a terrible impediment, but even then think of Helen Keller or Christy Brown. He was the tenth of 22 children of a bricklayer and his wife. Born almost completely paralysed except for his left foot, he was to turn his bad luck round and become as a writer an international best-seller. In such cases the handicap appears to act as a spur to achievement. That's the philosophy of the survivor, the one that future humanity is going to descend from.

"Being a scientist keeps me going. There are always so many interesting things to discover and interesting jobs to do."

DENNIS PICKERING

Dennis Pickering, 86 years of age, is a retired minister of the United Reformed church who lives with his wife Mary in Exmouth.

Dennis studied science before he began to think the Ministry was his vocation. I don't doubt that his popularity as a Minister was as much due to his friendliness and love of people as his open-mindedness. "Yes," he tells me, "my scientific education certainly encouraged me to question what I am expected to believe, but nonetheless my work as a Minister has been worthwhile. I enjoyed it and hope that it has been of help to other people. At the present time when many are searching for one or another form of spirituality, and although I am a Christian of the liberal, open-minded variety, I see our human lives in the perspective of evolution and the unimaginable scale of creation which is beyond our capacity to comprehend. I am excited by new discoveries of science in physics, astronomy, biology and so forth, and the challenges these present to our theological thinking. We live in interesting times.

"Science has encouraged me to employ my powers of observation, which have given me feelings of awe comparable with my passion for music. I have studied butterflies and moths, dragonflies and grasshoppers; many evenings you could find me photographing and recording the wildlife which teems around this place. Let me tell you about the time, early one morning, when I heard and recorded the song of a nightingale singing and singing in the dark. Wonderful! Quite marvellous! My religion encompasses such beauty, while accepting that life must prey on other life for its continued existence.

"I particularly love music; prayer and music are closely related. I pray more through music than through words. Messiaen's organ music, for example, says as much to me as the words of St John's Gospel. It seems to explore the mystery of the great Christian themes.

"My earliest memory of music is hearing Elgar conducting his overture, *Cockaigne*. But apart from Italian opera, I love the whole canon of Western music – early, classical, romantic and contemporary. Whenever I can, I'll go to the Edinburgh and Aldeburgh Festivals or whatever, to hear it interpreted by some of the finest contemporary exponents.

"Like all journeys, life has a beginning and an ending, which is an essential part of the evolution that has created us. Approaching the end of the journey, we must be prepared to find that our senses may become dimmed and our memories unreliable. We move more slowly, we encounter pain and discomfort as our bodies wear out after the burdens of the way.

"Perhaps it is that, as a minister of the Church and a former hospital chaplain, I have spent much time with the elderly, with people in pain, with the dying and the bereaved, that I have had to try to prepare myself for this time of my own old age.

"Yet there are benefits as well. Walking slowly now, I see and observe much that I did not notice when life's demands hurried me along. I have more time to read, to listen (with my NHS hearing-aids!) and to think. There is still so much to learn and discover. As a keen amateur naturalist all this means a lot to me (despite my poor breathing and painful arthritis). And with a family of whom I am justifiably proud I can look back with gratitude for all that life has given me. That helps me to face the frailties near the end of the journey."

ANNE WESTCOTT

Before I'd barely drawn a breath we were in at the deep end; here it was sink or swim. But Anne is like that: energetic, intelligent, yet perhaps a trifle scornful of those like myself who have difficulties in keeping up with her enthusiasms. "Yes," she exclaims, "ignore ageing. Ignore it altogether. Make the necessary provisions – the settlement of your house, for example – and then get on with living. Don't keep thinking about how old you are. Ignore chronological age altogether." In any event, after the age of 65 the State virtually ignores your existence altogether. Anne herself is 87.

Conversation with her is always a bracing experience. She has been a schoolteacher (History, English and a little Latin) for some forty years, and although she retains something of a sharp tongue, the abiding impression is of a friendly, even benevolent and far from old person: a mixture of energy, challenge and enthusiasm – which excites your interest. On this occasion Anne wanted to discuss her new-found fascination with a proverb which, she feels, may have something important to contribute to the subject of age: 'Those whom the Gods love die young.'

"For a start," she suggests, "let's look at the idea of youth. What characterises youth? Isn't it a condition of freedom, of flexibility, of open-mindedness and creativity? For, whereas old age summons up the idea of a person now fixed and set in their ways, youth makes us think about the promise of fresh possibilities. With youth we are eligible for happiness. Without it we can stiffen, set hard and cease to be responsive to the beauty and aliveness of the living moment. The spirit is infinite. Schubert died young – he was only 31 – but his music, the riches of his spirit, continue to influence the world every day of the year. No wonder the Gods love the young.

"Yes," she continued, "the spirit is the thing. The spirit flows through people and continues to do so after their deaths. Nothing is so satisfying to the human soul as creating something new. If the old can become creative in their own right, they are lost no longer. They experience rebirth.

"But to do so you must be prepared to keep an open mind and to have an activity that engages your heart. I used to run a dramatic society. The schedule for one year included Arthur Miller's *The Crucible*, W. B. Yeats's *Purgatory*, Shakespeare's *Much Ado About Nothing*, Albee's *The Zoo Story*, Sartre's *In Camera* and Pinter's *A Night Out*. But since those days and my retirement from teaching, I have moved to Appledore and opened a craft gallery in the first floor of my house. Choosing the pottery and paintings I am hoping to sell is a new and fascinating experience for me. The shop more or less breaks even and lets me enjoy the company of lots of people I would not otherwise have met.

"I am also interested in the science of man's occupation of Lundy, and am currently writing a paper for the Lundy Field Society on Neolithic Funerary monuments. Having been given some kind of intelligence, I feel under an obligation to make use of my gifts. But I also find enjoyment in a wide range of other things – I love keeping a garden, reading (especially detective stories) and carriage driving for an hour or two on a Sunday afternoon. I think of myself as a very fortunate woman – I've had so much fun, so many chances. Yes, getting older gives one a swelling sense of gratitude and freedom to experiment.

"I'm not a religious person in the conventional sense, but I certainly believe in the existence of a power greater than my own rather limited understanding of things. And since I can't even make a daisy, I feel bound to respect whatever it is that can."

CHAPTER NOTES

Introduction

The quotation by Jimmy Thirsk was from an interview by Becky Barnicoat in *The Guardian*, 21st February 2009.

A.E. Housman's poem was first published in *A Shropshire Lad*.

Chapter Two: A Short History of Ageing

The quotation on page 23 is from 'The Old Master', an interview of David Hockney by Tim Adams in *The Observer Magazine*, 1st November 2009.

According to the Office of National Statistics, in August 2008 there were 11.58 million pensioners (classed as men over 65 and women over 60), as compared with 11.52 million under-16s.

The UN expects population to stabilise at 9.22 billion in 2075. The United Nations Population Fund actually makes three projections for the year 2050: 7.6 billion and falling (the low estimate); 9.2 billion continuing to rise slowly to a peak near the end of the century (the medium estimate); and 11 billion rapidly rising.

'This looming crisis needs some grown-up solutions', article by Jackie Ashley in *The Guardian*, 14th December 2000.

For details about Rapamycin, see 'Secret of a longer life lies on Easter Island' by Michael McCarthy in *The Independent*, 9th July 2009.

Robert Butler is a noted gerontologist who recognised the discrimination being perpetrated against the elderly and coined the term 'ageism'. His books include *Why Survive? Being Old in America* and *The Longevity Revolution*.

Chapter Three: Coping with Ageing

The quotation on page 38 is from Lawrence Durrell's *Alexandria Quartet*.

Chapter Five: The Great Uncertainty

A survey conducted by Ipsos Mori in 2007 revealed that 54% of all men and 69% of women in this country believe that we have souls, and that 47% of all people believed in life after death.

Chapter Seven: The Art of Ageing

My Hero was published in *The Guardian* on 23rd January 2010. It was written about John Gross, the English author and literary critic, by his son, Philip Gross, a poet.

RECOMMENDED READING

On Ageing

Diana Athill, *Somewhere Towards The End*, Granta 2008.

Ronald Blythe, *The View in Winter Reflections on Old Age*, Allen Lane 1979.

Robert N. Butler, *Why Survive? Being Old in America*, Harper & Row 1975.

Robert N. Butler, *The Longevity Revolution: The Benefits and Challenges of Living a Long Life*, Public Affairs 2008.

Deepak Chopra, *Ageless Body, Timeless Mind*, Rider 1993.

Betty Friedan, *The Fountain of Age*, Jonathan Cape 1993.

Muriel R. Gillick, *The Denial of Aging: Perpetual Youth, Eternal Life, and other Dangerous Fantasies*, Harvard University Press 2006.

Glas, Norbert, *The Fulfillment of Old Age*, Anthroposophic Press 1986.

Leonard Hayflick, *How And Why We Age*, Ballantine Books 1994.

Carolyn G. Heilbrun, *The Last Gift of Time: Life Beyond Sixty*, Ballantine Books 1997.

Hermann Hesse, *Mit der Reife wird man immer jünger*, ISBN 3 458 34011 4.

Stanley Keleman, *Living your Dying*, Random House 1983.

Elizabeth Kubler-Ross and David Kessler, *Life Lessons: How our Mortality can Teach us about Life and Living*, Simon & Schuster, 2000.

Ni Maoshing, *Secrets of Longevity: Hundreds of Ways to Live to be 100*, Chronicle Books 2006.

Marian Van Eyk McCain, *Elderwoman*, Findhorn Press 2002.

John Cowper Powys, *The Art of Growing Old*, Jonathan Cape 1944.

Mary C. Morrison, *Let Evening Come Reflections On Ageing*, Bantam Press 1999.

Susan Moon, *This is Getting Old: Zen Thoughts on Ageing with Humour and Human Dignity*, Shambhala 2010.

Sherwin B. Nuland, *The Art of Aging: a Doctor's Prescription for Well-Being*, Random House 2007.

Ram Dass, *Still Here*, Hodder & Stoughton 2000.

Theodore Roszak, *America the Wise: The Longevity Revolution and the True Wealth of Nations*, Houghton Mifflin Company 1998.

Gary Small, *The Memory Bible*, Hyperion 2003.

William H. Thomas, *What are Old People For? How Elders Will Save the World*, VanderWyk & Burnham 2004.

Andrew Weil, *Healthy Ageing: A Lifelong Guide to Your Physical and Spiritual Well-Being*, Alfred A Knopf 2005.

Ben Weininger and Eva Menkin, *Aging is a Lifelong Affair*, Ross-Erikson, Inc, Publishers 1978.

Michael Young and Lesley Cullen, *A Good Death: Conversations with East Londoners*, Routledge 1996.

On Death and Dying

Peter and Elizabeth Fenwick, *The Art of Dying*, Continuum 2008.

Sue Gill and John Fox, *The Dead Good Funerals Book, Engineers of the Imagination* 1966.

J.B. Bradfield, *Green Burial*, The Natural Death Centre 1994.

Iona Heath, *Matters of Life and Death: Key Writings*, Radcliffe Press 2008.

Joseph Head and S.L. Cranston, *Reincarnation: The Phoenix Fire Mystery. An East-West Dialogue on Death and Rebirth from the Worlds of Religion, Science, Psychology, Philosophy, Art and Literature*, Warner Books 1979.

Elizabeth Kubler-Ross, *On Death and Dying*, Tavistock Publications 1970.

Sogyal Rinpoche, *The Tibetan Book of Living and Dying*, Rider 1992.

Stephen Wienrich and Josephine Speyer (eds.), *The Natural Death Handbook*, Rider 2003.

Felicity Warner, *Gentle Dying: The Simple Guide to Achieving a Peaceful Death*, Hay House 2008.

Other books

Stephen Bachelor, *Buddhism without Beliefs: A Contemporary Guide to Awakening*, Bloomsbury 1997.

Sarah Bakewell, *How to Live: or A Life of Montaigne in one question and twenty attempts at an answer*, Chatto & Windus 2010.

David Cadman, *Holiness in the Everyday*, Quaker Books 2009.

Irene Claremont de Castilllejo, *Knowing Woman: A Feminine Psychology*, Harper Colophon Books 1974.

Diana L. Eck, *Banaras: City of Light*, Routledge & Kegan Paul 1983.

Victor E. Frankl, *Man's Search For Meaning*, Rider 2004.

Erich Fromm, *To Have or to Be?*, Jonathan Cape 1978.

Dolf Hartsuiker, *Sadhus: Holy Men of India*, Thames and Hudson 1993.

James Hillman, *The Force of Character and the Lasting Life*, Random House 1999.

Timothy Hyman, *Bonnard*, Thames and Hudson 1998.

John Lane, *Timeless Simplicity: Creative Living in a Consumer Society*, Green Books 2001.

John Lane, *The Spirit of Silence: Making Space for Creativity*, Green Books 2006.

Peter Levi, *The Flutes of Autumn*, Harvill Press 1983.

Bruce Lipton, *The Biology of Belief: Unleashing the Power of Consciousness, Matter and Miracles*, Hay House 2008.

David Lorimer, *Survival? Body, Mind and Death in the Light of Psychic Experience*, Arkana 1988.

James Lovelock, *The Revenge of Gaia: Why the Earth is Fighting Back – and How We Can Still Save Humanity*, Allen Lane 2006.

Jeffrey Masson, *The Nine Emotional Lives of Cats: A Journey into the Feline Heart*, Vintage 2003.

David Maybury-Lewis, *Millennium: Tribal Wisdom and the Modern World*, Viking, 1992.

Suzanne Page, *Bonnard: The Work of Art: Suspending Time*, Lund Humphries 2010.

Jonathan P. Parr, *Death in Banaras*, Cambridge University Press 1994.

Kirkpatrick Sale, *Rebels Against The Future*, Quartet Books 1996.

Jean Yves Tadie, *Marcel Proust*, Viking, 1996.

ALSO BY JOHN LANE

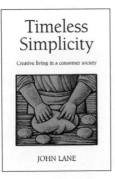

TIMELESS SIMPLICITY

Creative Living in a Consumer Society

"This is a real gem of a book, one that brings
a smile to my heart with its authenticity and
integrity." – Duane Elgin, author of
Voluntary Simplicity

112pp   ISBN 1 903998 00 7   £8.95 pb

THE SPIRIT OF SILENCE

Making space for creativity

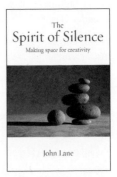

"In this gentle and inspiring book John Lane creates
the silence he longs for with the beauty of his words
and the weight and poise of his thoughts." –
Thomas Moore, author of *Care of the Soul* and
Dark Nights of the Soul

120pp   ISBN 978 1 1903998 74 8   £8.95 pb

TIMELESS BEAUTY

In the arts and everyday life

"I see this courageous book as marking the beginning of the end of the tide of materialism that has
prevailed for the last century."
– Kathleen Raine

176p   ISBN 978 1 903998 33 5   £9.95 pb

For a full list of books by John Lane published by Green Books, please see
www.greenbooks.co.uk. Most are also available in e-book formats.